*the book of*

# Daniel

*John H. Piersma*

 Reformed Fellowship, Inc.
3363 Hickory Ridge Ct. SW
Grandville, MI 49418

For information:
Reformed Fellowship, Inc.
3363 Hickory Ridge Ct. SW
Grandville, MI 49418
Phone: 616.532.8510
Web: reformedfellowship.net
Email: sales@reformedfellowship.net

Book design by Jeff Steenholdt

ISBN 978-0-9793677-2-4

# Contents

# Introduction

## The Book of Daniel

To provide a general introduction to these lessons we present here a brief summary of the main features of the Book of Daniel. We are indebted to the late Westminster Theological Seminary Old Testament scholar, Dr. Edward J. Young, and to Dr. William Hendriksen as our sources for this introduction. We take this opportunity to recommend Dr. Young's *An Introduction to the Old Testament* (Grand Rapids: William B. Eerdmans Publishing Co.) and Dr. Hendriksen's *Bible Survey* (Grand Rapids: Baker Book House).

Dr. Young groups his material under five heads: the name of the Book, the authorship, the purpose, an analysis of the contents, and the two languages which the Book of Daniel uses, namely, the Aramaic and the Hebrew.

The book takes its name from its author and principal character, Daniel. David's second son was also given this name (I Chr. 3:1), which means, "God is my judge." Daniel was a real, historical person (not, as some say, merely a legendary figure), who was born to a noble family in Judah, and was transported to Babylon by Nebuchadnezzar about the year 605 B.C., Daniel 1:1; Jeremiah 25:1. Ezekiel 14:14, 20 mention the same person.

Young declares that "it is the testimony of both Jewish and Christian tradition that Daniel, living at the royal court in Babylon, composed his book during the sixth century B.C." Hendriksen's view is not quite so dogmatic. The fact that the use of the third person with reference to Daniel occurs side by side with the use of the first person, 7:1; 10:1, and that in the entire historical section of the book, chapters 1–6, he is referred to in the third person is probably best explained by assuming that another inspired person collected the prophecies of Daniel and also wrote the narrative portion of the book. Proclamations by Nebuchadnezzar were also included in the book; see Daniel 3:29; 4:34–37; cf. 6:26, 27. This view of the matter is also in harmony with what is found in Daniel 6:28: "So this Daniel prospered in the reign of Darius, an in the reign of Cyrus the Persian," a statement which one would hardly ascribe to the "pen" of Daniel himself (p. 315).

The issue at stake is not whether the Book is to be regarded as written in its entirety as now found in the canon of Scripture by the hand of Daniel, but whether it could be composed in the sixth century, B.C. If it was composed that early its prophecies were wondrously *predictive*, written in advance of the things which are described. That this issue is important is stated by Dr. Hendriksen: If one accepts the theory according to which the prophecies which occur in this book are to be regarded as *vaticinia-ex-eventu* (predictions that grow out of the event), the question whether the book does not become a fraud cannot be suppressed (p. 316).

Although a detailed consideration of the argumentation is not possible or desirable here, a summary of Young's reasons for accepting the traditional interpretation may be helpful for anyone trying to understand this Book. Young lists four such considerations:

In Matthew 24:15 (compare with Dan. 9:27 and 12:11) Jesus Christ quotes from Daniel. Evidently Christ thought that at least a part of the Book came from Daniel himself. Young very properly points out here that if we attribute this to either ignorance or deception on the part of the Savior, we run the risk of rendering Him as something less than trustworthy. The consequences of such argumentation are too horrible to contemplate!

The testimony of Jesus Christ is validated by the claims of the Book itself. The prophet speaks in the first person and claims to have received Divine revelations (for example: 7:2, 4, 6ff.; 8:lff., 15ff.; 9:2ff.; 10:2ff.; 12:5–8). In 12:4 Daniel is ordered to preserve the Book. Young argues that "if Daniel is named as the recipient of the revelations, it follows that he is the author of the entire book." He sees the following as arguments for the unity of the book:

1. The structure of the Book is logical in pattern. The first part prepares for the second, the second looks back to the first. Chapters 7–12 develop more fully the vision of chapter 2, and none of these is intelligible without chapter 2.

2. All the various parts of the Book interlock and depend upon one another, even within the two main sections. This can be seen by comparing 3:12 with 2:49; the removal of the sacred vessels prepares for the understanding of Belshazzar's feast in chapter 5; 9:21 should be examined with 8:15ff.; 10:12 with 9:23, etc.

3. The historical narratives of the first six chapters uniformly serve the purpose of revealing how the God of Israel is exalted over the heathen nations.

4. The character of the author is consistently and uniformly the same throughout the entire Book.

5. Scholars of divergent schools of thought have acknowledged the literary unity of the Book. In addition to conservative scholars, such men as Driver, Charles, Rowley, and Pfeiffer have regarded Daniel as a unit. In Matthew 10:23; 16:27ff.; 19:28; 24:30; 25:31; 26:64 the New Testament gives at least indirect approval to the genuineness of the Book of Daniel. Historical objections to the references to the Babylonian and Persian empires do not seem to be valid.

This is a sketchy indication, of course, of the way in which the authenticity of the Book has been argued by Bible believing scholarship. Anyone who cares to read the careful consideration given by Young of alternate views of authorship may find this on pages 353–364.

Purpose: Hendriksen's theme for the Book is "God's Sovereignty in History and Prophecy." Young says that "the Book of Daniel seeks to show the superiority of the God of Israel over the idols of the heathen nations. In the latter days the God of heaven will erect a kingdom that will never be destroyed. Daniel, then, may be said clearly to teach the sovereignty of God in His dealing with human kingdoms." In our first outline further refinements of these ideas will be suggested.

Analysis of the Contents: An overall review of the twelve chapters of the Book of Daniel will be helpful to us in our study.

**Chapter 1:** Places us in the center of the stormy sea of nations about the time of the death of Judah's great king, Josiah, concerning whom Jeremiah wrote his song of mourning. Josiah was the king whose death is as the setting of the evening sun for Judah, gloriously splendid, but marred by a background of threatening storm clouds. Chapter 1 introduces us to the entire Book, giving us to see Nebuchadnezzar as he besieges Jerusalem and brings a group of the sons of the nobility to his court. Among them are Daniel and his three friends. Their first conflict has to do with the appointed food of the king, and by God's wonderful power they are made to excel over all others.

**Chapter 2:** Nebuchadnezzar sees a colossal image in a dream, and this troubles him no little. Daniel is able to describe and interpret the dream when all others fail. The image is interpreted to represent four kingdoms, marked by the limitations of their human origin, temporal character, limited scope. Just exactly in the time when these rule with all the force and cruelty of a wicked, imperialistic lust for power, the God of heaven will establish an eternal, universal Kingdom. The four kingdoms are perhaps best interpreted to refer to Babylon, Medo-Persia, Greece, and Rome, respectively, although the scope of this prophecy goes far beyond these four kingdoms.

**Chapter 3:** In this chapter we are told of the courage of Daniel's friends, Shadrach, Meshach, and Abednego, who dare to refuse to obey Nebuchadnezzar's order to kneel before the great image. When these heroes of faith tell Nebuchadnezzar that their trust is in God, he, enraged, orders them cast into a fiery furnace which is so hot that those who carry out his orders are killed by the heat. In the furnace the king sees these men unharmed and accompanied by a Fourth. Nebuchadnezzar thereupon orders them to come out of the furnace and praises their God.

**Chapter 4:** Again Daniel is brought in to furnish the interpretation of a dream which Nebuchadnezzar's wise men were unable to tell. The dream is fulfilled upon the king who is made to suffer from insanity for a time. Upon his recovery he recognizes and praises Daniel's God.

**Chapter 5:** During an impressive feast in the court of King Belshazzar, a miraculous writing appears upon the wall of the palace. Daniel offers an interpretation as a warning of doom to the king. The warning is fulfilled, and Belshazzar meets with death.

**Chapter 6:** The successor to Belshazzar's throne is Darius the Mede. Certain jealous rivals of Daniel plot to destroy him as they get the king to establish a law making it absolutely illegal to pray to any other but the king. Daniel refuses to obey this law, of course, and is cast into a den of lions from which he is miraculously delivered by God.

**Chapter 7:** Daniel sees four monsters in a dream which occurs during the first year of Belshazzar's reign. These beasts represent the same kingdoms as the image of chapter 2. There is enlargement, however, upon the revelation of chapter 2. It is here shown that the fourth kingdom has a threefold history, for on its head are ten horns which symbolize ten kings or kingdoms. These represent the second stage in the beast's history. A little horn arises which upsets three of the ten horns and speaks great things against God, making war with the saints. However, as in chapter two, God erects a Kingdom, eternal and universal, which is given to the heavenly Figure like a Son of Man. When at last the little horn seems to have defeated the saints of the Most High, God intervenes, and the fourth beast is entirely destroyed, the saints receiving the Kingdom.

**Chapter 8:** Daniel sees in a vision under the symbolism of a ram and a he-goat the destruction of the Medo-Persian Empire by Greece under Alexander the Great. When Alexander dies the kingdom is divided, which fact is represented by the four horns. From one of these four a horn emerges that begins small but grows very large. This horn is Antiochus Epiphanes, who opposes God's people in a terrible manner. At last he is cut off radically.

**Chapter 9:** Daniel reports that he has studied Jeremiah's prophecy concerning the seventy years of exile. He offers a prayer of penitence to God, confessing the sins of his people. Gabriel answers Daniel's prayer with the well-known prophecy of the "Seventy Weeks." The general idea is that a period has been decreed for the accomplishing of the Messianic work. This Messianic work is described negatively and positively. Negatively: restraining the transgression, completing the measure of sin and covering iniquity. Positively: bringing in everlasting righteousness, the sealing of vision and prophet, and anointing a holy of holies. In this chapter Daniel is given and reveals a prophetic perspective with respect to the Coming of Christ.

**Chapter 10:** A divine message is revealed to Daniel in which we see that the angelic hosts do battle in defense of the Church on earth. This serves as an introduction to chapters 11, 12.

**Chapters 11, 12:** These are very difficult chapters, perhaps the most difficult of the entire Bible! They depict the wars between the kings of Egypt (Ptolemies) and those of Syria (Seleucids). The rise of Antiochus Epiphanes is described, and his Egyptian campaigns as well as his most severe persecution of the people of God. The rise of Antichrist and his warfare is also presented. Daniel is ordered to seal up the Book and the prophecy is ended.

The Two Languages of the Book: Chapters 2:4 to 7:28 are written in the Aramaic language, the rest in the Hebrew. What is the reason for the use of the two languages? Young comments:

> There does not appear to be any truly satisfactory explanation of the two languages. The explanation which seems to be freest from difficulty is that the use of two languages was deliberate and intentional upon the part of the author. Aramaic was used for those parts which dealt primarily with the world nations, and Hebrew for those which treated principally the future of the Kingdom of God. This view is surely not free from difficulty, but on the whole it appears to be the most satisfactory (p. 367).

"Between the seventh and second centuries B.C.E., the world saw the rise and then the collapse and disappearance of six great world empires: Assyria, Babylon, Persia, Macedonia, the Seleucid and Ptolemaic kingdoms. With them died their religions and their culture, leaving behind an indelible imprint on the civilizations that were to come. Throughout all the changes of this time of upheaval, the Jews survived, a distinct cultural and religious entity, indestructible in the face of all vicissitudes."[1]

With these sentences the impressive volume, *Daniel to*

*Paul,* opens its description of "the period up to and beyond the New Testament, including the intertestamental literature (the Apocrypha and Apocalypses), the sectarian writings of Qumran, the historical background of the Hasmonean and Greco-Roman periods in Palestine, and the new evidence about the War of Bar Kosba recently discovered in the Judean wilderness."[2]

It is at the opening of this period that Daniel writes his prophecy. By it the faithful were given assurance of the triumph of the Kingdom of God — a faith that was tested and strained unbelievably by the events of that cruel, godless era.

It is still true today that the faithful will have to learn and re-learn the perspective of the Book of Daniel if they are to survive until the End!

---

1. Gaalyahu Cornfeld, ed., *Daniel to Paul, Jews in Conflict with Greco-Roman Civilization: Historical & Religious Background to the Hasmoneans, Dead Sea Scrolls, the New Testament World, Early Christianity, and the Bar-Kochba War.* 1962. New York: The Macmillan Company, pp. 1, 2.

2. *Op. cit.,* p. ix.

# God's Indestructible Kingdom

*Daniel 1*

## Introduction

Our plan is to cover Daniel in a series of twelve outlines. Those who require more than twelve lessons will find it profitable, perhaps, to devote two discussion periods to each chapter.

The general title, "God's Indestructible Kingdom," is intended to say that the Kingdom of God is shown in this Book to be able to survive and triumph even though the most impressive of the world's kingdoms always decay and fall. They that have a true faith in the King of that indestructible Kingdom possess "the victory that overcometh the world" (I John 5:4b), even today!

No possible substitute could be urged for anything but a careful, repeated reading of the Book of Daniel itself! For that, neither these outlines nor any other book is a replacement, but may be seen as mere aids. For an English commentary of sterling, conservative quality we recommend Edward J. Young, *The Prophecy of Daniel* (Wm. B. Eerdmans Publishing Co., Grand Rapids, Mich.).

## Jerusalem vs. Babylon

Jerusalem and Babylon are mentioned in the very first sentence of this Book (1:1). These cities represent the Kingdom of God and the kingdoms of this world or the kingdom of Satan, respectively. These are in God-ordained (Gen. 3:15) opposition to one another. This opposition is often called *the antithesis*. This antithesis is due to an irreconcilable conflict between two different spiritual principles. This conflict penetrates to the depths of every human heart, and extends to every manifestation of temporary life: science, culture, politics, economics.

The Book of Daniel indicates plainly that the deepest source of our attitude and viewpoint with respect to life's most basic questions is not some scientific theory but the actual *religious* posture and motive of our lives.

Please note that Babylon seems to be in control here. It was the great city in the great kingdom built by the brilliant young Nebuchadnezzar upon the ruins of Assyria and its capital city, Nineveh. Babylon is the first of the great monsters which Daniel sees emerging from the turbulent waters of the history of that time. Spiritually, Babylon stands in the tradition of Nimrod (Gen. 10:8), is the center of unbelief, the proponent of salvation by its own power and in its own way. Babylon reaches out to seize Jerusalem and the People of God. Although at first concessive, in about fifteen years both city and temple are destroyed, throne and altar are removed, and the flower of the nation deported. This is God's judgment upon the sin of David's house, the infidelity of the Aaronic priesthood, the idolatry of a covenant-breaking people.

Domination by the world is not normal for the City of God! Jerusalem is the center of faith, the city of David, "God is in the midst of her" (Ps. 46:5), the city of sure protection and wondrous deliverance by God through grace. It is not because Jerusalem cannot survive or conquer in this world that she is defeated and destroyed, but because she does not care to utilize in covenant obedience and love the resources found only in the Word and grace of God.

It is not, however, the intent of this Book to focus attention upon the citizens of Judah and Israel. God is not indifferent to their plight (as can be seen from the fact that

He raised up three great prophets in the time of Israel's Captivity: Jeremiah, whose task is to preach to those who remained behind in Judah; Ezekiel, who worked among the exiled people of God; and Daniel, whose "parish" is the Babylonian palace). The Book of Daniel reveals that the God of the Scriptures is the King of the kings of the earth, and that the Kingdom of God is indestructible and therefore everlastingly victorious. This is the same Kingdom which is to be fulfilled in Jesus Christ, the Head of the Church (Matt. 28:18; LD 19, Q/A 50, Heid. Catechism). This emphasis can be seen from the fact that the Book of Daniel seldom uses the covenantal name for God (Yahweh), and uses repeatedly those names which reveal Him to be the Most High, the God of heaven, the King of the kingdoms of this earth, the God who is the ruler of history.

The nature of the Captivity can be compared to a temporal excommunication. His service was cut off, His people were cast out of their inheritance, the covenant blessing was displaced by God's curse until the end of His wrath should be accomplished. The sacrifices of atonement and reconciliation ceased, the Mosaic temple service was terminated, the Davidic kingdom of peace was lost, God's kingship over His people seemed entirely absent. There was neither throne nor altar for Israel and the loss of these is fatal!

It is just then that the world powers arise. As bulwarks of Satan they emerge in forms more powerful, more fearful than ever before. They are indeed shadowy precursors of the very Antichrist himself. In them the contours of the man of sin (II Thess. 2:3ff.) are more sharply drawn than ever before. But here is a principle which we must see to understand the work of the God of history: *When the light is extinguished in Jerusalem, then the dark depths of hell come into view.* We see such hellish depths in our own time, and the biblical perspective by which we can understand the reason for their appearance demands that we look at the world from the vantage point of a recognition of the ever-gaining apostasy. The church has doused its light, and the flickering flames of hell's ungodliness and lawlessness is a miserable substitute.

It is just then that God presents Himself as the One who has not abandoned His people. He has, on the contrary, accompanied them into Babylon, and established Himself in the very palace of Nebuchadnezzar. There He will demonstrate His royal power, that power which is redemptive for His own, at the same time a terror for His enemies. God does this not only in terms of a spiritual comfort for His children, but also as the actual King in the very political life of this monstrous Babylonian dictatorship. Political life belongs to Him, and He will not allow it to be taken away from out of His control. Temporarily He has given His own over to the Babylonian beast, but this is not because He has capitulated, but because His people have preferred to be like the world rather than to live as the peculiar, antithesis-conscious people of God.

A very important part of this antithetical struggle concerns the youth of the church. Daniel 1 pictures this in a very deliberate and striking manner. In addition to the holy vessels taken out of the Temple, several holy young people (I Cor. 7:14) are brought to Babylon. The intention was to "Babylonize" God's own peculiar and holy people, to erase their spiritual distinction by dealing with them as if they were just another of the several kinds of people, of no essential difference from the heathen. We would say today: these representatives of God's heavenly people were to be made worldly so that they could adjust well to their new environment. A primary intention, of course, was to break their will to resist as a captive people.

Why did Babylon's powerful rulers fasten their attention upon such young fellows (about fourteen years of age)?

And why did they choose this representation from Israel's royal family and nobility? There are several obvious reasons:

1. The world rarely takes lightly the importance of the younger generation.

2. The world understands that youth are indeed impressionable, and that they can, of all groups, be most readily influenced and changed.

3. The world understands that particular attention should be directed toward the more gifted since they will soon occupy positions of leadership in life.

Daniel 1 mentions three ways in which the effort is made to drench Israel's elite youth in the spirit of *heathendom* (meaning: the world of the non-Christian religions as fallen away from and opposed to the one, true God, and as addicted to the idolatrous pursuit of security and happiness by finding a oneness with the forces of the cosmos). These three ways are:

1. **Education:** verse 4 indicates that these lads are to be trained so that their biblical, Jewish religious ideas will be replaced by the thought patterns of the Babylonian world.

2. **Identification:** verse 7 shows that everything, even their names, which might remind them of the God of Israel (the name Daniel means, "God is my judge") had to be effaced.

3. **Religion:** (by *religion* we mean the practical system of faith and worship). Their daily menu (cf. vs. 5, 8ff.) was so designed as to make them forget the Jewish laws regarding diet. All of the features of the lifestyle of their forefathers must be rejected.

From all of this it is easy to see that a well-designed system had been devised to bring about a break with all things that would remind them of and keep alive the old religion, "the faith of the fathers."

The faith and wisdom of Daniel and his three friends appear in the fact that they saw through the satanic objective, namely, the gradual weaning away of God's children from Him and His service. It is tragic that this is to be found in these four only. The large majority of their class in Babylon's court seems to have capitulated right from the start. It may be supposed that they found the attitudes of Daniel and his friends to be highly exaggerated and unnecessarily rigid. Still more, it is noteworthy that especially Daniel not only "stopped the mouths of lions" (Heb. 11:33) when he was cast into the lions' den, but that he was also alert to the presence and threat of the satanic forces as he moved among the privileged in the luxurious salons of the king's palace. The danger at the king's table was just as much as that in the lions' den.

One could say it this way as well: the *practice* of godliness comes up for decision and application in the most ordinary things of everyday living.

It is crucial to the understanding of Daniel 1 to recognize that the issue at stake in the matter of the food and drink prescribed by Nebuchadnezzar was indeed important. Nothing appeared on the table of the king which had not first been consecrated to the gods of Babylon. When Nebuchadnezzar deposits in his temple the sacred vessels stolen from Jerusalem, and when he urges upon Daniel and his friends the royal diet, he is in both instances denying the true God, and involving these young men in this denial. For the warfare between Jerusalem and Babylon was raging across the entire range of human life, extending right down to the very food required for the sustenance of life. It is amazing and encouraging that God's Holy Spirit was able to make the king's servant willing to try Daniel's suggestion. This was not only contrary to his religion, but also extremely dangerous for his personal life and well-being! Imperialistic despots do not usually show much tolerance for acts of disobedience. But God triumphs in Babylon's temple by making one of Nebuchadnezzar's disciples perform this act of disloyalty.

Daniel's faithfulness is rewarded by God with long life (v. 21). Daniel continued to the first year of Cyrus which is the year of liberation for Israel. Daniel survives even the removal of the kings and the nations. He is typical of the Church which, although violently attacked, remains until the return of Christ. This kind of security is for all who, like Daniel, stay with and stand upon the Word of God. The victory of Christ over Antichrist is certain, as can be seen from this chapter, in which we see that God really maintains Himself and His own right in the presence of and in opposition to the king of the golden empire, Nebuchadnezzar.

**Questions for Discussion**

1. Are there any obvious parallels between the features of modern life and those of the life which Daniel and his friends were drawn into in Babylon? For example: Does the world today try to erase from our consciousness the awareness of our distinctiveness as people of God? Do today's Christians really dare to assert that they are something special and different as God's people?

2. Is there any relationship between the ordinary things of earning a living today and our Christian testimony? Can a Christian really obscure his position without actually compromising that position in today's society?

3. Is it required that we raise the issue, like Daniel, at the seemingly indifferent point of our daily diet?
Isn't Daniel really too serious and too religious? Should we train our children to be that careful about things?

4. Daniel 1 reveals that the believer is to be found right in the very arena of the world with its antithetical, spiritual struggle. Why is the word antithesis all but lost among us? Do we really desire to show our true colors in this struggle by, say, building Christian schools, or are we merely in the grip of a pious tradition which is in danger of being replaced by a desire for schools "of superior academic and moral quality?"

# God's Indestructible Kingdom II

*Daniel 2*

## Introduction

Daniel 2 might be called the overture to the drama of world history as described by the prophet. In it, the Great Maker of History gives us in a single, quick projection taken from His secret counsel a brief but nevertheless comprehensive look at the course of history with respect to its scope, meaning, and purpose. This is done very simply in a dream! Only God could give us such a short, all-comprehensive, true, and easy-to-understand vision.

In Daniel 2 we find, therefore, an introduction to the rest of the Book, and a revelation which is necessary to the understanding of history as interpreted by this Book. Although we have no quarrel with the interpretation which identifies the four principal sections of this dream with Babylon, Medo-Persia, Greece, and Rome, our viewpoint is that in this chapter we have a description of the true nature of all imperialistic kingdoms based on worldly considerations rather than the Word of God. This viewpoint we would work out in this lesson, drawing lines, therefore, which reach into our own time and circumstances, and which speak to us concerning our calling as believing Church members in today's world.

### The Dream and Its Interpretation Unrest and Panic in Babylon!

Daniel 2 tells us of things which probably took place in the twelfth year of Nebuchadnezzar's reign. His star was still ascending even though a great portion of the Near East was already under his domination. Daniel and his friends are now about twenty-one years of age.

We go along with authorities such as Aalders that the reference to "the second year of the reign of Nebuchadnezzar" is at fault since it obviously conflicts with the statement in chapter 1 that Daniel and his friends were to undergo a three year period of training. There are other possible ways to explain such things, of course, but it would appear that we cannot go out from the idea that Daniel 1 represents the first year and Daniel 2 the second year of Nebuchadnezzar's reign.

The dream of Nebuchadnezzar of the great image which is destroyed is not an ordinary but a *revelational dream*. God gives this monarch to see how transitory his kingdom is. Apparently Nebuchadnezzar felt that this was the case early in his reign. And this awareness makes him restless and uneasy. It seems as if he had not retired restfully, but that he was bothered with "thoughts of what would be hereafter" (see v. 29). This was not a consideration of life after death, but of the future of his kingdom. Apparently he did not regard the political prospects of Babylon to be altogether favorable. The dream attached itself to these dark and disturbed thoughts. Kings are always sensitive to harbingers of danger, and so the dream and its interpretation became a matter of utmost importance.

In his anxiety, perplexity, and insecurity Nebuchadnezzar seeks help from the sources of *human wisdom*. The king's uneasiness is reflected in the haste with which he summons his advisers before him in the royal chamber. The soft light of hundreds of lamps glowed in the darkness of a night not yet spent as row upon row of "magicians, astrologers, sorcerers, and Chaldeans" stand before the great (and capricious) king. These were the men who claimed to possess the holy art of divining the secrets of the gods. Nebuchadnezzar shocks them by demanding not only the interpretation of the dream, but the telling of the dream itself without information from the dreamer.

The request of the king is not altogether unreasonable, nor unfair, even though it might seem that way at first glance. There is dictatorial arrogance in this request, of course, but despots are always marked by such conduct. Nebuchadnezzar has not forgotten the dream, but he is uncertain as to whether he can really trust his wise men. The whole situation is one of frightening anxiety, and these sly, clever men know that their very existence depends upon the whim of the king. Don't forget, these men maintained as their boast that they owned a special relationship to the gods, and so the dream itself as well as the interpretation should be available to them. It would seem as if Nebuchadnezzar had been disappointed by his wise men before, but this time he senses that the significance of his dream is so great that he cannot risk deception.

The wise men cannot furnish the test of the dream, and their acknowledgement of this fact causes the king to order their mass execution. The unrest and confusion in the capital city of the great Babylonian empire intensifies. We see a repetition of this kind of disturbance and anxiety in our own time. Today, for example, modern man is very upset about the possibilities for destruction and calamity resident in his own inventions. Vainly he looks for the world of wisdom, as did Nebuchadnezzar. A straight line can be drawn from the unrest and panic of Daniel 2 to that of our own day. We also see that prosperity and strength do not bring peace and security, but fear and distrust and disquiet.

### The Restfulness of Faith

We do not know why Daniel and his three friends were not present in the palace when the king had his unsuccessful conference with the wise men. Perhaps they were not members of a particular religious order in Babylon, perhaps they were not available when the hasty summons was issued. At any rate, they are among those ticketed for death by the king's decree (people like Nebuchadnezzar have little concern for such details as the presence or absence of a particular victim of mass execution).

Daniel's reaction is notable for its wisdom, sobriety, and restfulness. He gains audience with the captain of the king's guard, and with prudence and discretion discusses with him the nature and the reason for the king's severe decree. At this point Daniel requested formally of the king an appointment for an interview in which he might show the king the interpretation of his dream. Please note that this appointment is sought before he has the revelation from his God! This is faith.

The first constructive thing that Daniel did when he learned of the desperate situation he and his friends and his colleagues (supposedly!) were in was to *pray*. He and his friends did that which is quite characteristic of the Church when they brought their need to the Lord (Phil. 4:6, 7), and pleaded with Him for *mercy*. Their motive is not simply preservation of life, but the desire not to perish with a group which had been exposed as untrustworthy and deceptive. God's people do not belong in that kind of company.

When it comes to the welfare of the Kingdom of God and His Church, no prayer is ever too much! Humanly speaking, they asked an impossible thing, namely, the revelation of that which was known only to the mind of the king. Even after it was given them by the Lord they would have to trust God to so work in Nebuchadnezzar's heart that he would acknowledge the truth of the revelation as well as agree to its interpretation. After praying they go to sleep (God's answer came to Daniel while he was asleep). The righteous can sleep even when the sword of a cruel and arbitrary despot hangs over their heads. Note the contrast between Nebuchadnezzar's unrest and Daniel's quietness, between the different effects of faith and unbelief.

### God's Revelation to Daniel

Daniel's prayer is answered by God with clear and unmistakable revelation of both the dream itself and its infallible, divine interpretation. His first reaction is praise to God (vs. 20–23). This does come first, even ahead of saving one's life! In this doxology Daniel shows us that this dream and this Book have to do with "the times and the seasons" in which God "removes kings and sets up kings." In true prayer God's glory is always the first consideration.

After thanks and praise to God Daniel goes to the captain of the guard to ask him to tell the king that he has the knowledge that the king desires. Here another Christian principle is revealed: when we have that which God has told us as revelation of His will, then our making known of that will is for the preservation of others. For it is not to impress Arioch that Daniel says, "Do not slay the wise men of Babylon," but to indicate that he is the one who alone can save them from impending disaster. The pattern of true prophecy always reveals the activities of the Christ, our chief prophet, whose prophecy is the only sure word of salvation.

Note that Daniel is introduced by a liar. The captain of the guard says that he has found someone who can make known the interpretation the king desires. This is indicative of the lying atmosphere in which Daniel labored as a prophet of truth, and of the fact that truth is always opposed by the counter claims of him who is a liar from the beginning, even the Devil.

It is important to notice how Daniel begins his address to the king. He declares that only God in heaven could possibly reveal and explain the dream, that the dream was indeed a revelation of God to Nebuchadnezzar, and that he is merely the instrument of God in this instance. This is the necessary prophetic humility and self-denial (vs. 27–30).

The perspective of the dream's interpretation reaches all the way to the end of time. As we have said, the identification of the golden head with Babylon is obvious, of the breast and arms of silver with Medo-Persia, the belly and thighs of bronze with Greece, and the legs of iron with Rome is likely. The difficulty comes, however, when we consider the feet of iron and clay. Without detailed explanation, we suggest that the dream means to say that there is a real difference between the first four kingdoms and those represented by the feet and toes with their iron and clay composition. The difference lies in the fact that after the Roman Empire the kingdoms of the world are marked by a more pronounced attempt at synthesis of all the different elements of race, ideology, social, and political institutions, religion, etc. The reference is to the New Testament age in which monolithic empires such as the first four is not the dream, but rather the composite, truly world-wide empire of social and spiritual amalgamation in the way of synthesis.

It would appear that the Bible is telling us that these attempts at world organization will be marked by hardness (cruelty, ruthlessness, especially with respect to God's people, the people of the *antithesis*) and weakness (the attempt to synthesize all these different backgrounds, races, ideas, religions does not ever really succeed). The hardness is represented by the iron, the weakness by the clay, of course. (Please take note of the reference to mixed marriage, v. 43.)

There is only one real union of all the peoples of the world, and it is in Christ, the King of the everlasting Kingdom, pictured as "a stone... cut out by no human hand." It smites the whole image, and reduces it to powder which blows away as the chaff of the threshing floors. Please note that every last vestige of the world's kingdoms will be destroyed. One might wonder if this does not do violence to the suggestion that the "true, the good, and the beautiful" found in the world will be preserved and ultimately brought into the Kingdom of Heaven. We must not forget that whatever these kingdoms possessed of such truth, goodness, and beauty was there only because of and through Jesus Christ. It never was indigenous to the heathen mind or culture as such.

The amazing thing in this chapter is the reaction of Nebuchadnezzar to Daniel's account of the dream and its interpretation. How would you like to tell such a king such a story? Daniel knew what he was doing, and he did it, not to gain prestige with the king, surely, but because he was ordered by his God! Disregarding self, he gains everything in God's service: the recognition of his God as supreme (Nebuchadnezzar kneels before him!), elevation to high office, promotion for his brothers, wealth, personal honor, etc. This is evidence of the power of the Word, which overcomes every anti-christian bulwark, and accomplishes that which God intends it to do.

### Questions for Discussion

1. Is it in conflict with our high view of the infallibility and inerrancy of Scripture to try to solve the kind of difficulty posed in connection with the reference to the second year

of Nebuchadnezzar's reign (v. 1)? What is the difference between "lower" and "higher" criticism of Scripture?

2. What is the true nature of biblical wisdom? Is wisdom a natural endowment? Can wisdom be had by all Christians (James 1)? How does wisdom rank with other Christian characteristics? Is it really important to be wise?

3. In chapter 1 we saw the existence of the all-pervasive antithesis between the cause of God and the world. How does the antithesis make itself known in chapter 2? Doesn't Daniel ignore the antithesis by his concern for his fellow, unbelieving wise men?

4. Is there a reflection in today's world of that which is said of the kingdoms of clay and iron? Is there a difference between the foot and the toes in this vision (note that in v. 41 the clay is mentioned first, in v. 42 the iron receives first mention)? Can you see anything prophetically in the fact that life is reported to be dull and gray and monotonous in such places as Moscow?

*Lesson 3*

# Delivered Out of the Fiery Furnace

*Daniel 3*

## Introduction

Also in this chapter we must see the struggle between the Kingdom of God and the kingdom of the world. Although the Kingdom of God realizes a singular triumph here, a total breakthrough in terms of the true service of the one and only God among the heathen is not achieved. Nevertheless we can see the beginnings of that which is fulfilled in the adoration of the newborn Christ by the wise men from the East, and of that to which Paul refers in Philippians 2:10.

## The Image in the Plain of Dura

It is striking as well as typical that a man like Nebuchadnezzar would erect a colossal image in the plain of Dura even though he had said earlier that "God is a God of gods, and a Lord of lords" (Dan. 2:47). This, too, is striking confirmation of the biblical emphasis upon the need for regeneration rather than mere reformation.

Everything would seem to plead for the idea that this image was a representation of Marduk, Babylon's chief god, rather than, say, a statue of Nebuchadnezzar himself. The great consecration service for this image was a religious affair, although in terms of Babylon's false "theology." The Babylonians were astrologers, that is, believers in the theory that the gods revealed themselves in the stars. Astrology is heathenish, and quite, contrary to the biblical teachings of the providence of God when it suggests that one can know what is happening and will happen by studying the relative positions of the stars.

Very simply, the great religious event of which chapter 3 speaks is an ecumenical feast in which representatives of all parts of the empire are present to declare that Marduk, the god of Babylon, is "the lord of the gods." For this reason the colossus is placed in the plain of Dura, in the province of Babylon, and all the nations of the empire are "invited" to be present for its dedication. Its size is impressive: about 108 feet in height, 10.8 feet in width. Very likely it was based on an elevated foundation which one would ascend by climbing many steps. This provided a stage on which the king and his favorites would be enthroned.

Although the primary character of this great consecration service for the image of Marduk is religious, its occasion is the fact that under Nebuchadnezzar Babylon's military might has triumphed everywhere. Please note that the base number is *six*. The image is sixty cubits high and six cubits in breadth. This is similar to that which we read in Revelation 13:18. The anti-Christian movement in history is apparent here, and as such demands without hesitation that it be given that recognition due only to God. In the image built by Nebuchadnezzar the power and prestige of man is exalted, and this calls for nothing less than public worship.

The praise and worship of man is stimulated and maintained only by much drum-beating, by intensive and extensive "promotion." Everybody who is somebody is summoned. All the devices of worldly propaganda are brought into play. Candid reckoning is made with the fact that everyone present is not one hundred percent in agreement with the entire program. All who kneel are not doing so voluntarily, and Nebuchadnezzar realizes that. Therefore the burning oven, the fiery furnace. Its presence is a warning to all that the religious demands of the king of

Babylon are for real. This entire project rests upon fear and force. Be sure to take note of the contrast: Nebuchadnezzar's rule rests upon compulsion and fear, but the service of God in His Kingdom is a service of love, freely, gladly given.

## The Fiery Furnace

Daniel's friends, Shadrach, Meshach, and Abednego, for conscience' sake, refused to pay homage to the image. Why Daniel was not present we do not know. The drama of that moment in which three men dare to defy the emperor's order is something anyone can imagine! When the signal is given, after careful and explicit instruction, everyone kneels, except these faithful sons of the Most High God. Right in the face of an antichrist do they refuse to pay divine honor to any but the God of Israel.

In every dictatorship one finds a Gestapo-type of person and organization, and Babylon is no exception. Representatives of this kind of group bring the three friends to account before the king. In addition to the fact that totalitarian governments are always concerned with rebels and traitors, we must take note of at least a pair of additional factors:

1. *Racism*: In their accusations against these three men the Chaldeans place repeated emphasis upon the racial identity of these men as Jews. This is an early evidence of anti-Semitism. Anti-Semitism has its spiritual roots in the fact that the Jews were God's particular people. The New Testament church inherits this hatred in its time.

2. *Jealousy*: The designation in verse 12, "There are certain Jews whom thou hast set over the affairs of the province of Babylon," is quite transparent. These Chaldeans could not endure the fact that Jews had been placed in such high positions of authority. They were nationalistic as well as racistic, jealously working to

keep the glory and the power in the hands of "our people." The glory of Israel was not racial or national but spiritual. It was the glory of God's grace which was intended to radiate from Israel over the whole world.

The temptation in this situation arises when Nebuchadnezzar reveals his affection for the accused. He provides them with an "out" by asking if their conduct was intentional or unintentional. Had they perhaps forgotten, or had they been so overwhelmed by the grandeur of the occasion that they failed to kneel? Nebuchadnezzar offers them a second opportunity to demonstrate their loyalty and obedience, and if they will go along this time, everything will be forgotten. Imagine the pressure on these men now as they face this crisis! If the king, no less, is so concessive, so fair, and so decent, why not go along "just for once"? After all, does our salvation really depend on such insignificant things as a quick curtsy before a worthy representative of God's ordained power?

Take note of their answer, verses 16–18. It is brief, strong, and clear. Its message is that they are not concerned with personal safety but with the honor of their God. Therefore they are not afraid to answer, for they are certain that if his honor is served by their deliverance from death in the fiery furnace, he is able to provide such deliverance. And if God is not minded to deliver them, their allegiance remains unchanged. They love God, and serve Him because they know Him to be the one, true God, and so they are not really influenced by the consequences of their faith or by the possibility of miraculous deliverance. This is a mighty testimony to the real nature of faith in and love for God!

Please notice that the three friends reply in such a way as to posit the antithetical opposition of God to the false gods of Nebuchadnezzar. There were possibly other ways of witnessing which might have been more tactful, less direct, more diplomatic. These are all abandoned because the three friends truly understand that the issue is not personal or political or a matter of professional welfare (they were recognized political figures in Babylon with much to lose!), but a religious issue in which the matter of faith in the God of heaven and earth or the false gods of Babylon is at stake.

There is little we can add to what the chapter says about the miracle of the preservation of his Church in the fiery furnace. We would be quite superficial, however, if we failed to notice that *there is a greater miracle in this chapter than the fact that these men emerged from the furnace unharmed.* That is the miracle of God's preservation of his own in the Babylonish world. The answer of these men reveals that they had not been overcome by Babylon's culture, philosophy, view of life. This is not to be attributed to their faithfulness and steadfastness and devotion to truth but to the sovereign grace of God!

**The Mysterious Fourth Party**

God speaks to the heathen in his own language by placing a heavenly figure in the furnace with the three friends of Daniel. It is indeed true that help must come from heaven, but not from the stars. It must come from God of heaven and earth. Note, too, that the revelation of God is indeed in terms of Immanuel, God with us. Nebuchadnezzar sees these four walking about, an expression which means that they were not only safe from the fire but that they were also enjoying the life of Covenant communion with God, even in that place.

There is some question as to whether the angelic figure seen is the Angel of Jehovah, or the Old Testament revelation of the Son of God, our Lord Jesus Christ. Certainly it is a foreshadowing of Him, at least. And He is the One who has come to save us from the fire that is never quenched, the fire of hell.

We must not forget that deliverance out of temporal difficulty depends upon the question as to whether such deliverance is for God's honor. Shadrach, Meshach, and Abednego remind us that our faith precedes such deliverance, and reckons fully and fearlessly with the possibility that it might not please God to intervene miraculously. Still more: the Church and the Christian must realize that in the kind of day in which anti-Christian forces such as Nebuchadnezzar rise and rule many believers will be slaughtered and oppressed. The Book of Daniel reminds us to be sober and watchful.

In the apocryphal books one can find a prayer supposedly offered by the three men while in the fiery furnace. Noteworthy is the fact that they do not make complaint against Babylon for placing them in this awful situation, but blame themselves and their people for their previous practice of idolatry with the followers of Baal.

## Nebuchadnezzar's Tribute of Praise

This story ends with a doxology spoken by Nebuchadnezzar. It is followed with a royal proclamation guaranteeing absolute safety to the three men, and threatening death and destruction for all who speak anything against their God. This is a remarkable reversal! This whole thing begins in terms of man's wicked desire to glorify man (you have noticed that Nebuchadnezzar really identifies himself with his gods, asking, "do ye not serve my gods, not worship the golden image *which I have set up?*" (v. 14), but it ends with praise to God.

It would have been better, of course, if Nebuchadnezzar had cut in pieces the image which rose above the plain of Dura instead of threatening to do that to any who said anything against the God of Shadrach, Meshach, and Abednego. That the image remains standing indicates that

Nebuchadnezzar's "conversion" was one which was only in words, and not in deeds.

**Questions for Discussion**

1. Why does it seem impossible for men to leave "religion" out of their activities, even while they are talking about tolerance, broadmindedness, and the need for world-wide cooperation?

2. If one angel could reduce Nebuchadnezzar to such consternation, what will be the effect when the Son of God comes in all His glory to reveal the full power of the eternal Kingdom?

3. If the greatest wonder in this chapter is the fact that Daniel's three friends did not succumb to the spirit of the world in which they lived, how can we who are even more seriously threatened by worldly culture today escape its influence?

4. Why doesn't the world learn even when it is given to see such demonstrations of the power of God and His Kingdom as is revealed in Daniel 3?

# Nebuchadnezzar's Proclamation

*Daniel 4*

This chapter is a royal proclamation which begins with the salutation of verse 1, sets its theme in the doxology of verses 2, 3, and 37. The jubilation of one who has been desperately ill and is now restored to health and dignity is reflected in these words. The king's joy is so great that he does not shrink back from public notice "unto all people, nations, and languages, that dwell in all the earth." It is not typical for despots so to expose themselves!

The story is told in the first person, except for the section found in verses 26–33. This does not make dubious the fact that Nebuchadnezzar is the author of this proclamation for 1) the things told in that section took place outside of his consciousness, and 2) we have a similar use of the third person in a command of David (I Kings 1:33) and a letter of Artaxerxes (Ezra 7:11–26).

The obvious intention of the proclamation is to bring rest and confidence to the people. Although the element of praise to Daniel's God is very striking, Nebuchadnezzar's proclamation is very self-centered. His own rehabilitation is its primary concern, and he wishes all people to know that they can have the most complete assurance that things are well with the world now that he has been restored to health and power.

We accept the view that the illness and restoration of Nebuchadnezzar took place late in his career. After he had succeeded in building up his empire and its marvelously impressive cultural and political center, Babylon, in something of world renown, and just when he anticipated the satisfactions of a well-earned retirement *he meets God.* It is only in a dream, and yet its effect is to make one of the greatest rulers the world has ever known to be terribly afraid. For God had decided that this representative of the world's lust for world empire should praise Him. The same man who had destroyed Jerusalem and its Temple, who had triumphed over David's House, who had brought the people of God into the shame of captivity would sound the praises of Israel's God in the ears of the whole world.

The salutation, "Peace be multiplied unto you" (v. 1) is, in the light of the entire prophecy and its antithetical nature, to be seen as an example of the fact that in history the issues always concern Christ and Antichrist, the true and indestructible Kingdom versus the kingdoms of men-based always on false claims and false hopes and doomed to destruction. In spite of the outward friendliness of Nebuchadnezzar to God and his anointed prophet, Daniel, these lines of demarcation remain.

### The Dream of the Great Tree

Although Daniel is the titular head of the company of the wise, he is consulted last. If the world can make it without help from God it will always prefer to do that. Daniel is, of course, extremely busy, since he is not a professional wise man but a prophet of God whose primary concern is God's will and calling for his life. He has, therefore, to be summoned from "behind his desk" as an in-service, highly-placed government official.

The problem presented to Daniel is not so much the dream as its interruption by a heavenly emissary with his startling pronouncement calling for the hewing down of the great tree. Nebuchadnezzar had dreamt of himself as the one under whose rule and protection all creation-found peace and provision. This was a very proud dream. That the dream was to be interpreted as something which had to do with a particular person is evident from the fact that the stump of the tree was to be a man of bestial mind and habits.

Daniel's interpretation is clear and direct — as Christian prophecy ought always to be. He tells Nebuchadnezzar that the great tree is himself, that because of his pride he is threatened with that which the angel announced, and that he ought therefore to repent by a deliberate return to the practice of justice and a demonstration of mercy to the oppressed. "Justice" and "mercy" usually suffer at the hands of the world's despots, and the consequences are hard for "the people," that is, those who are not within the ruler's inner circle of favorites. Nebuchadnezzar is given a gracious postponement of divine judgment, but he does not avail himself of this opportunity (of course not, for he is not wise unto salvation). A year later that which the angel had, announced comes to pass. Very suddenly he is afflicted with insanity. We picture the situation this way: God's agents from heaven reach down to bring God's decree into execution. Very dramatically, in a moment, the great king becomes as a raging animal, and all the skill of Babylon's experts cannot help him. He is given over to the wilderness, where he seeks the company of the wild beasts, whose manners he adopts and whose appearance he resembles. This lasts for seven years.

A very instructive glimpse of the task and character of the angels is given in this chapter. Please note in verse 17 that they are deeply involved in the carrying out of God's will. God's will is something which they honor and implement with deepest satisfaction. They understand the warfare which lies behind the scenes in Babylon, and which is the key to its real meaning.

The first evidence of the removal of God's judgment is indicated when the Bible says that "Nebuchadnezzar lifted (his) eyes unto heaven." This is prayer, or, at least, the acknowledgement of God. Then sound reason returned to the king. And then God elicits from this humiliated man a tribute of praise. In that tribute Nebuchadnezzar speaks of God's everlasting dominion and kingdom. This is what the Book of Daniel is all about: the Kingdom of God which even Babylon cannot destroy.

It is noteworthy that Nebuchadnezzar's tribute makes no mention of God's grace and mercy, nor does it give evidence of confession of guilt out of a smitten heart, broken by that knowledge of sin which is learned in the light of God's Law. Nebuchadnezzar was and remains a heathen who speaks about the most High God, but does not use His Covenant Name, nor does he desist from speaking of Bel (v. 8) and of "the holy gods." Nebuchadnezzar was not a David. Nebuchadnezzar confesses only because God has overcome him. He is not broken by God's grace but humiliated by God's power. He is not "a nice man" who has respect for the religion of other people, but a defeated warrior who could no longer hold out against a greater opponent.

Then Nebuchadnezzar receives his kingdom back. How this took place we are not told. We find it most acceptable to imagine that his son ruled during his illness with the assistance of Daniel, and that when his father was restored to health the throne was given back to him. It is a remarkable situation in which we see a man who for seven years was written off as hopelessly insane restored to a position of highest prestige and authority in all the world. Fact is that his position is enhanced and his power increased after his restoration.

This, too, was from God. Was it a reward? Not in the least. There was nothing for God to reward, since there was not a shred of that kind of good work which is out of faith in God. The reason for all of this is to be found in the emphasis which is made in this chapter on God's sovereignty. God does realize His purposes, and "He doeth according to His will in the army of heaven, and among the

inhabitants of the earth: and none can stay His hand"
(v. 35). Thus the restoration of Nebuchadnezzar is a part of
that divine providence which is not only preservation and
cooperation but also *government*, that is, the realization by
God of that which He decrees. God had determined that He
would be praised and the remnant of His people comforted
by the most unusual and unexpected tribute of praise by a
great world-ruler. That is the explanation for this happening.

Although this chapter is a royal proclamation written by
an unbeliever, we are convinced that it is an integral part of
the infallible Word of God. The fact that the Spirit of God
is the actual writer of Scripture guarantees for us the
historical reliability of the Bible. There are other people
whose words are taken up in Scripture whose unbelief we
cannot ignore: Balaam, for example, and Caiaphas, and
possibly Agur and Lemuel in the Proverbs. It must be
remembered that the question is not whether these were
true believers, but rather this, are their words the Word of
God? It does not depend in the Bible upon the inspiration
of the *person* but of the *words* spoken by them, regardless
of their faith or unbelief, their personal understanding or
misunderstanding, or their intentions. God has even used
the heathen in the writing of His Word. And thus in
Nebuchadnezzar's proclamation a word of God went out to
the peoples.

We might quickly review the development on the theme
which this prophecy preaches. This theme is the
indestructibility or invincibility of the eternal Kingdom of
God. This is an assurance we need because all Christians
are taken up into that Kingdom, and are delivered from the
kingdom of the world. In the great struggle of these
kingdoms they are not only comprehended but are
also asked to suffer and endure hardship and pain.
Three revelations of this truth of the indestructible Kingdom
we have seen so far:

1. In chapter 2 God reveals to Nebuchadnezzar that he is the head of gold, but that an everlasting kingdom, the Kingdom of God, will triumph. The prophet of this Kingdom lives for years among the Babylonians, and although they are happy to exploit his skill and wisdom, they do not believe his preaching.

2. In chapter 3, God reveals to Nebuchadnezzar that His Kingdom is a kingdom of grace and deliverance out of the power of death. This, unlike the revelation of chapter 2, takes place publicly in connection with the miraculous preservation of the three friends in the fiery furnace. But again Nebuchadnezzar does not repent of his sins.

3. This third revelation in chapter 4 reveals the overwhelming power of God's Kingdom as it humiliates the king by a direct intervention of heaven.
Now Nebuchadnezzar pays tribute to the Most High because he is compelled to do so. There is a logical progress in all of this. It ought to move us to godly fear as well as suggest to us the only true comfort!

### Questions for Discussion

1. What can we learn from the fact that an unbeliever such as Nebuchadnezzar can see so much of God's great working in history, can say so many good things in praise of God, can show so much appreciation for the people of God, and still does not yield to the grace of God?
2. Why is Nebuchadnezzar allowed to wander about so pitifully among the animals in the wild without kind, sympathetic care as an elderly man and an important person? Does this indicate that modern concern for the

insane is something which has its origins in the Christian religion and its viewpoint?

3. In Nebuchadnezzar human cultural aspiration reached one of its greatest heights (read somewhere a description of the glory of Babylon). What is God saying as to the end result of humanism and its strivings when we are given to see the almost too revolting picture of a king who turns into a beast?

4. Does one really have to be a citizen of the Kingdom of God to be a Christian and to be saved? If so, why is there so much preoccupation today with the soul and human need rather than the biblical idea of an all-embracing Kingdom of God? Is it more important to have personal assurance and comfort than to labor for the coming of His Kingdom (or: does assurance come in the way of such effort)?

## Lesson 5

# Babylon's Glory Declines

*Daniel 5*

**Introductory Remarks**

Chapters 5 and 6 form the conclusion to the historical section of Daniel's book. In these chapters (5, 6) the circumstances and the times are quite different from those in chapters 1–4, where we read repeatedly about Nebuchadnezzar. In chapter 5 Belshazzar is in control. Belshazzar is not the son but the grandson of Nebuchadnezzar, who was a son of Nabonedus. The queen mentioned here is Belshazzar's mother. It is likely that she was a daughter of Nebuchadnezzar.

Daniel is to be seen here as an elderly man whose great accomplishments and contributions of the past are all but forgotten. It is about thirty years after his appearance in the palace described in chapter 4. After Nebuchadnezzar's death Daniel seems to have been lost in the multitude of bureaucratic servants which great governments seem always to create. We must remember that Daniel is not primarily a government official but a believer in God and a servant of His Word. This Word is to be spoken on behalf of the God of the Word, and in this instance it meant a long time of patient waiting until his faithful servant was once again brought before the king and his guests to fulfill his prophetic task. They who do the Lord's work must often wait long for His time!

The feast arranged by Belshazzar took place at a very late and very dark moment in his reign. His enemy, Cyrus, had already captured everything but a small part of the city of

Babylon, a section which by virtue of its stout military defenses had escaped capture. It is hard to believe that a king so obviously endangered would still find it possible to celebrate, but that is what he did. Is this, perhaps, a scene reflective of the world's persistent dream of safety and success, no matter what?

Although the Chaldean-Babylonian empire is replaced by the Medo-Persian, the struggle between the Kingdom of God and the anti-Christian kingdoms of this world continues. The cast in this great drama changes, but the spiritual issues under dispute remain the same. In fact, we see an actual *intensifying* of the hostility. In chapter 1 the effort is made to destroy the Church by way, of cunning and guile (by "Babylonizing" Israel's elite youth), but in chapter 3 we see the use of raw physical power in the case of the fiery furnace. Looking forward to chapter 6 we find the world putting forth its most vigorous and dangerous attack by trying to take away the Church's greatest and last weapon, prayer. Nevertheless, the LORD's kingdom emerges from the fray victorious. His Name comes to be known among the heathen, and is even lauded in the official documents of the imperial government.

### The Sin of Belshazzar

The sin of Belshazzar is idolatry (v. 23). The seriousness of his idolatry is to be seen against the background of his grandfather's humiliation as recorded in chapter 4.
As indicated above, the time of this idolatrous, wicked feast is marked by war, a war which has seen all but total disaster for Belshazzar and his friends. Here the world shows itself to be unconcerned so far as the warnings of God are concerned, an unconcern which persists even today when the signs of the Lord's return for judgment are very plain.

The depth of human depravity is always shocking beyond description! This is to be seen on this occasion especially when the golden vessels originally taken out of the Temple at Jerusalem are used in the service of the Babylonian gods. You must not forget that the Babylonians were very broadminded, so to speak. They honored all gods of all peoples, even subject nations. And they were afraid to desecrate things dedicated to the gods, no matter what they thought of the people to whom these kinds of gods belonged. Their actions here are the deliberate expressions of contempt for and hatred of the Almighty God. Even in the very face of destruction and annihilation the wicked find pleasure in pouring out their scorn upon the One, Holy God.

Daniel's sermon before the king and his assembled guests (vs. 17–24) is most courageous, as is all true prophecy. True prophecy is always marked by complete fearlessness so far as its apparently inevitable consequences are concerned. Who can imagine saying such things to an oriental despot, without being killed? Daniel knows very well that this isn't the way to save one's own life, but he is not out to save his own life. And so he tells the king such very hard things as:

1. Nebuchadnezzar's rule is to be understood as something which came from God, the God of the Jerusalem temple.

2. Nebuchadnezzar's sin was pride, that is, refusal to recognize God as the one by whose appointment and in whose strength he might rule.

3. Nebuchadnezzar's period of humiliation was something brought about by Daniel's God.

4. Belshazzar could have known all this, but refused to humble his heart, preferring to worship the gods of silver, gold, brass, iron, wood, and stone.

5. Belshazzar must now expect God's wrath in judgment.

The severe reaction of the king and his party to the sudden appearance of the hand of God as it writes upon the palace wall is not to be attributed to anything but the fact that it is *God's hand* which has appeared. Babylonian kings were quite used to seeing things which were interesting and arresting and even awesome, but these things do not make them feel so undone as verse 6 indicates. Once again, how terrible will be the Day of the Lord, when every eye shall see Jesus Christ returning in glory to judge the living and the dead! Still more: Belshazzar is so troubled by a few words written by God. Why aren't we more troubled by a whole Bible full of warnings and admonitions, all of which are likewise written by God's hand?

God troubles Belshazzar. The pathway to the "peace that passes understanding" leads over the way of that kind of disturbance which God works by His Word of warning. God's warnings are always merciful, even when they come at such a late moment as the one our chapter describes. It is, indeed, too late to prevent the destruction of Babylon, but not too late to urge Belshazzar and his company to bow before Jerusalem's great God. Men must know that God rules in the kingdom of men, and that He establishes and removes whomsoever He pleases. He alone is God, and His Kingdom is the only indestructible kingdom. Everyone will know this eventually, of course, but the wise will understand now and be saved.

The sign written on the wall is not decipherable by the wise men of Belshazzar's kingdom. Again, this must be understood spiritually. These experts were well-trained, gifted, respected men whose accomplishments were by all merely human standards outstanding. But God reveals to His children in their humility and simplicity that which is hidden from the worldly wise.

The Queen-mother hears of the confusion in the banquet hall, and comes to investigate. She remembers Daniel, God's prophet, and advises that he be summoned to interpret the writing on the wall. We have mentioned the fact that Daniel had apparently gone into obscurity. We must bear in mind that Babylon's greatness was directly involved with Daniel's presence in that kingdom. For the sake of Daniel, and because of his sanctified rule as a chief in Babylon, God had allowed that anti-Christian kingdom to grow and exist. But the world always forgets the source of its strength and success, and so now Babylon must come to its destined overthrow.

We would miss a great deal if we would not see here the fact that the Word of God is involved in and determinative for everything in life, *even politics*. Political life is not something with which spiritual life has nothing to do. When politics is treated as if it were something from which Christians may keep themselves aloof, then it must become secular in character, that is, concerned only with gold, silver, brass, iron, wood, stone — the things which represent human advantage apart from God's real blessing in Jesus Christ.

We think that the sign written by God on the wall was actually composed of just the first letters: M M T P P. To Daniel was revealed both the words themselves and the interpretation. The words, "mene, tekel, and upharsin," are the names of weights (literally, a pound, a sixtieth of a pound, and two halves of a sixtieth of a pound). These stand for numbering or counting, weighing and dividing. The "interpretation" (the miraculous unfolding of something secret) applies to the destiny of Babylon. God has counted Belshazzar's kingdom and has decided to put an end to it (*mene*). God has weighed the kingdom and found it to be deficient (*tekel*). The word *upharsin* is the plural of *peres*, which resembles the name *Persia*. The idea is that God is predicting and working both the breaking of Babylon's rule and the handing over of the kingdom to the Persians.

Belshazzar's reaction to Daniel's prophecy is not given in much detail. Evidently the obvious truthfulness of that which was revealed by the elderly Jew was so overpowering that he could not but recognize that it was indeed the correct answer to his question. It seems that he did what many do when they hear the Word preached, that is, applaud the preacher but refuse to believe and practice what is said. The proper response to God's Word is not to say, "What a gifted preacher," but to say, "Amen."

We ought to see a very plain reference to our Lord Jesus Christ here. Daniel is made "the third ruler in the kingdom." This means that he is the most important man after the king and the king's father. This might have been a great honor if Belshazzar's kingdom were not all but defeated. The reference to our Lord lies in the mockery which this represents. Daniel predicts the downfall of Babylon, and as a reward he is given a high title in that which he has, from God, revealed and exposed as quite worthless. Expired kingdoms are not very valuable. So our Lord was mocked when He served as our chief prophet while on earth.

That very night Belshazzar was killed and the new rule of the Medo-Persians is installed under Darius. The fall of Babylon is predictive of the fall of the Antichrist (Rev. 18). Like Babylon, the kingdoms of this world will come to naught because "in her was found the blood of prophets, and of saints, and of all that were slain upon the earth."

## Questions for Discussion

1. Why did Belshazzar make use of Jerusalem's holy vessels, while none had done so before in Babylon?
2. Do you recognize the hand of Satan in this chapter, especially in the rejoicing of the king and his party on the eve of Babylon's destruction?
3. How do we account for the consternation which follows upon the mysterious handwriting on the wall, and the unbelief and indifference which both precedes the appearance of the hand and follows the interpretation by Daniel?
4. How do you understand the description of Daniel as prophet found in verse 12?
5. Was there really an opportunity for Belshazzar and his followers to be saved from their sin in this preaching of Daniel?
6. How does this chapter make plain the fact of the sovereignty of God in history?
7. Point out the points of conflict between Babylon and Jerusalem in this chapter; what do these mean?
8. Why is the anti-Christian world in Revelation 18 compared to Babylon?

# By Faith Daniel Stops the Mouth of Lions

*Daniel 6*

## Introduction

In chapter 6 we find the presence of a new world empire, the Medo-Persian, with Cyrus as "ruler of the world." Although the Babylonian Empire has been defeated, things aren't really much different — to the naked eye — in the great city of Babylon. Babylon was a great trade center, and in spite of Persian conquest remained a powerful and prosperous financial capital for many years of the Persian supremacy. It was "business as usual" in Babylon.

Cyrus appoints Darius the Mede as king of Babylon, an important post because of that city's economic influence (and "money talks," indeed!). Darius is probably the same as the one called Gobryas. He served Nebuchadnezzar's regime as a politico-military leader, but seems to have gone over to the Persians in the time of the inept Nabonedus, father of Belshazzar. He was a capable, serious man, and there is reason to believe that the citizens of Babylon were glad for the change which brought him to their beautiful and important city as king. He is not a young man, having reached the age of sixty-two years (ch. 5:31).

Appearances were deceiving in Babylon at this moment, however, for God's prophetic and incomparably powerful curse had been pronounced upon her. In just a few years her role as a royal city was ended, and within a few decades her walls were broken down. Babylon, whose pride had made her think of herself as the queen of the whole earth was doomed to a slow process of decay and decline. God had determined to bury her greatness under the desert sands in order that his people might always know that only His Kingdom is indestructible!

## The Attack Upon Prayer!

As we have said, Darius is a more competent and more earnest man than his predecessor, Belshazzar. He is an able organizer and administrator (cf. v. 2), dividing his realm into 120 districts with three presidents, one of whom is Daniel. It takes but a little while and Daniel comes to the top as the very best of the presidents and the other district governors because "an excellent spirit was in him." In our opinion we must not be afraid to recognize this as the indwelling Spirit of God, by virtue of which Daniel is wise, fair, and scrupulously honest. Since the great task of the governors and presidents is to administer the tax program, such qualities were both necessary and appreciated. We must not forget, of course, that integrity and righteousness are not typical of bureaucrats in a worldly empire.

The character of the opposition to Daniel is the familiar staff jealousy often seen in life. This is not its deepest nature, however. It is another example of the bitter anti-Semitism or hatred for the Jew which we see so often in the Book of Daniel. This is not simply because "Jews are rich" and "Jews are smart," but because they were representatives of God's electing grace. Sinful man cannot be reconciled to the thought that God is sovereign in the dispensation of His grace!

The Bible says that the governors and presidents were unanimous in their desire to get rid of Daniel, whose skill and excellence they could not endure. Their first attempt is to find something faulty in his daily work. Surely he is not perfect, and especially in a position in which one has to entrust many things to subordinates there ought to be some evidence of incompetence or dishonesty. This attempt fails miserably, because Daniel was, says the Bible, *faithful*. This means that Daniel did his work diligently, obediently, energetically, sincerely. He knew that a believer must also be faithful in the pursuit of his daily calling.

Then his enemies resolved to try something else. They would bring Daniel to disgrace and death (they knew that their efforts really constituted murder) by taking advantage of his piety, that is, his uncompromising devotion to his God and his faith. They knew that Daniel observed the practice of regular prayer. They knew that he was especially fervent in this practice because of his passionate interest in them who had returned to Jerusalem, who were even then busy to restore the City of God to its rightful position in the world. Daniel had not returned with the others because his God had things for him to do in Babylon, but his heart was with them. The plot was simple: Get the king to pass a law which would make Daniel's religious exercises illegal, and one could count on his stubborn determination to do the things of his — in their opinion — ridiculous religion anyway. This would mean death for him, since law for the Medes and Persians was unchangeable and absolutely compulsory.

Even though Darius is very fond of Daniel, it becomes apparent that the real situation in Babylon has not changed. It is still the battleground between Jerusalem as City of God and Babylon as City of the World (Gen. 3:15). Darius seems to have fallen for the suggestion of his rulers without much effort on their part. The idea that none might perform an act of religious devotion for thirty days as an expression of loyalty to the crown is flattering, and he translates this evil suggestion into law. The trap has been set!

Prayer is the heart which pumps life and power for and into the Church, and so this attack is not a small matter.

If the world could really close the mouths of believers, it would succeed to destroy the cause of God. It was the intention of Daniel's competitors to remove Daniel from his place of leadership. Behind this. desire lurks a sly and deceptive Satan, whose purpose it is to shut up one of those righteous men whose supplications are unbelievably effective (Jas. 5:16). If this satanic objective is reached God's people would be lost. For Daniel was in the world as one of God's favorites, even as Job had been, and God blesses these because of their pure and uncompromising love for Him. Still more, the pathway to heaven did lie over Jerusalem, the City of God, where he had chosen to dwell and from where he was pleased to dispense his blessings. Satan was trying to cut the tie between God and His people.

The greatest miracle of Daniel 6 does not take place in the lions' den. It is that Daniel perseveres as a praying prophet, and as a praying intercessor. He is, therefore, a "type of Christ."

**Persistence in Prayer!**

Verse 10 tells us that when Daniel heard of the king's decree with its attendant threat of punishment he hastened to pray. This is for two reasons:

1. He was a believer, or, as we would say today, a Christian. A Christian always prays. One can no more compel a believer to give up prayer than one can command the thunder to remain quiet. Prayer is natural for the believer.

2. Daniel was not of a mind to compromise his position before God. He does not give way to the kind of thinking which begins to speculate as to whether we ought to do right "when it won't do any good"or still worse, "when we can preserve our future testimony by remaining quiet for a little while" (in this case, just

thirty days). Daniel knew that his prayers would bring about his personal downfall, but he offers them anyway because he can do nothing else.

Not only does Daniel find it impossible not to pray, even if it should cost him his life, but he is also humble enough to pray. We must not forget that throughout his life this man of God has been honored with the highest honors men ever get in this life. To illustrate, there is little doubt but that Daniel knew a measure of authority and power which few in our time ever see. Nevertheless, he prays! He prays because he knows that he is but a child of God, and that he is nothing apart from God, and that whatever he might lose in the pursuit of God's service is as nothing compared to the reward of the faithful.

### Victory Through Prayer!

By his fervent, sincere prayer Daniel overcame the world of his time! It might have seemed to be otherwise, for he is spied upon by his enemies, found to be in conflict with the unalterable law of the Medes and Persians, brought before the king, and sentenced to death. The horrors of a cold, heartless, unbelieving formalism are to be seen here, when we see a king compelled to sentence to death someone that he knows is not worthy of such punishment. Again: a reminder of Jesus Christ and another representative of a worldly empire, Judge Pontius Pilate of Rome. Neither Darius nor Pilate dare to do what is right.

Daniel's downfall is in appearance only. In the first place, Daniel is the only one whose mind is at rest. His attackers are deeply troubled, knowing that they have perpetrated raw injustice. And his judge, King Darius, is so unhappy with the situation that he lost a nights sleep on account of it. This is a primary result of true prayer, namely, peace of mind when everyone else, even one's most hostile enemies, are upset.

The second fruit of Daniel's prayer is that his faith stops the mouths of the lions (Heb. 11:33). This is the faith which is "assurance of things hope for a conviction of things not seen" (Heb. 11:1). This faith knows God as the Creator of heaven and earth, and releases the power of the only God when it is required for the coming of His Kingdom. An angel was dispatched by God to restrain the lions, because His servant Daniel had prayed. In his prayer he had pleaded innocence (v. 22), which means that he asked God for help upon the basis of God's promise to provide a "great high priest" (Heb. 4:14). God's answer to Daniel means that He recognizes that those who trust in Him because of the promised salvation in Christ are perfectly righteous, indeed.

Things do not necessarily turn out as they did with Daniel. God is also honored by the martyrdom of His saints, and we are not to expect anything but that He will do that which the glory and well-being of His Kingdom requires. It was God's desire that the annals of this anti-Christian empire should contain a testimony to the supremacy of the God of the indestructible Kingdom, and therefore the lions could not consume Daniel. If we expect that everyone and anyone will be delivered according to his prayer, we will be expecting more than He has promised.

The victory included exposure and destruction of God's enemies as well as Daniel's deliverance. This is something which reminds us of the final judgment. In it, too, the unbeliever will be exposed as one who hates God and rejects His Son, Jesus Christ, and his treatment will be accordingly. Let us be sure to believe on the Son of God, lest we share in such a destruction!

## Questions for Discussion

1. Was Daniel right in his willingness to obey a worldly ruler representing an ungodly empire?
2. Does this chapter teach that we may disobey certain laws laid down under certain circumstances by the government?
3. Should we also pray with our faces set toward Jerusalem?
4. How must we evaluate Darius' assurance to Daniel that God would take care of him in the lions' den?
5. How must we account for Darius' keen interest in and love for Daniel?
6. Should not Daniel have interceded with the king to spare the lives of his enemies? Was it right to include their families in this punishment?
7. Do you think that any of Darius' subjects came to saving faith through the proclamation of the king (vs. 25–27)?

# Bird's-Eye View of History

*Daniel 7*

## Introduction

With this chapter we go on to the prophetic section of the Book of Daniel. We do not have a chronological arrangement, since in chapter 7 to the time of Belshazzar. The character of the last six chapters is different from that of the first six. But the *theme*, the subject discussed, is the same. Here, too, we are placed before the ever-sharpening *antithesis*. That was revealed to us historically in the first six chapters. In the last six it is described in prophetic terms so that we are given to see the declining glory of the world powers and the ever-enduring luster of the Kingdom of God.

## Daniel's Dream in Chapter 7

Chapter 7 contains Daniel's dream about the successive world empires. This does not mean that we are given a lesson in what is called *general history*, since Daniel sees the development of these kingdoms in the light of *prophecy*. By *prophecy* we mean that he is given to see the program and the meaning of their history in terms of their relationship to the indestructible, certain-to-come Kingdom of God. Of that glorious Kingdom these kingdoms are radical, deadly enemies. The *thesis* (that which is set forth as Truth) of God's Kingdom is the profession of faith in Him and His redeeming grace, while the *thesis* of the world's kingdoms is that of the profession of faith in man and his own ability to work out his personal and collective salvation by his own power. These are not merely competitors, but unqualifiedly hostile to each other!

The sea which Daniel beholds in his dream is the sea of nations, that great sea which is always in turmoil. The Bible asks us to look at the restless sea and from it to form our understanding of the character of history as decreed by the sovereign God. This turmoil we must expect! Out of that turbulent sea Daniel sees the emergence of four awful beasts or monsters. These are representative of the successive world empires. That nations or empires are represented by beasts or birds is familiar (the Russian bear, the American eagle, the British lion, etc.).

It is important to see that the perspective of chapter 7 is not limited to the actual kingdoms indicated by the four beasts. The Great Judgment of the "Ancient of days" (v. 9) indicates that we must see in this chapter something which has real meaning for the Christian church throughout the current New Testament dispensation. In our opinion, that which is sketched here is to be seen as going through a double fulfillment. The first is that which runs through the four kingdoms unto the crucifixion of Jesus Christ, the second which runs through the final manifestation of Antichrist and the glorious return of Jesus Christ as Judge in the last day.

There is a noticeable difference between Nebuchadnezzar's dream (ch. 2) and Daniel's dream. Nebuchadnezzar also saw the succession of worldly kingdoms in the impressive image of gold, silver, and other metals. That was, so to speak, a humanistic dream. In it the glory of man is exalted, even though the true interpretation exposes the transitoriness of man and predicts his certain downfall. Daniel, on the other hand, sees the kingdoms of the world in a soberly biblical fashion, and then their representation is that of the ravenous beast. At bottom the imperialistic accomplishments of sinful men are not noble or humane, but bestial, cruel, harsh, oppressive. The succeeding kingdoms increase in cruelty and inhumanity as time marches on.

There is good reason to identify the lion with the Babylonian empire, the bear with Medo-Persia, and the leopard with the Greek-Macedonian kingdom. The fourth is identifiable with the great Roman Empire, but it is so unique that we discuss it separately under a second main head. These kingdoms represent an ever-increasing imperialism. The empires depicted are progressively more aggressive. We must not delimit the prophecy of chapter 7 to these kingdoms, however. This is evident from verse 12 which states that the lives of the first three "were prolonged for a season and a time." Their spirit goes on until the very end of time.

To make our point as clearly as possible in chapter 7 we see the nature of history from Daniel's day to the very last day of Christ's return in glory for judgment. The chapter gives us "a bird's-eye view," with all the advantages of such a view, but also with its limitations. The great feature of that history will be the appearance and reappearance of the imperial monster, the incurable desire of man to subdue the whole earth according to his own rebellious and wicked and godless desires. Of this imperial, beast-like, awful thing the kingdoms of Babylonia, Medo-Persia, Greece, and Rome are representative types.

## The Fourth Beast

The appearance of the fourth beast (vs. 7, 19, 23, 24) is just another part of Daniel's dream, but it requires, in our opinion, separate treatment. Our reason for doing so is that the chapter itself repeatedly *distinguishes* the fourth beast from the other three. We have identified the fourth beast with Rome, which, in the light of Revelation 17:9 ff., is quite obvious. However, this must not be taken to mean that the Roman Empire is the total significance of the fourth beast. Let us say again, chapter 7 is not to be understood as anything less than a bird's-eye view of all history from Daniel through Christ to Antichrist and the Great Judgment of the last day.

Terror, dread, and awful power are depicted by the fourth monster, which is nameless because of its unbelievable horror. It devours, crushes, tramples to bits all that comes in its way. But the remarkable thing about this beast is its horns. There are ten, and these are said to be kings which rise out of the fourth beast. And these are followed by still another, different from the rest, whose power is so great that three of the others are eliminated by him.

Our interpretation of this is that the fourth beast represents the last of the anti-Christian world empires, and that its spirit and character dominates all history until the end of the New Dispensation. Thus the number ten is to be seen symbolically to mean the fullness, the complete number of all imperialist kings in our time, and the eleventh king, the one that is altogether different (v. 24) is to be seen as the great Antichrist of that time just before the end.

The character of the Antichrist is vividly and fearsomely described. In general he is distinguished for his avowed opposition to God, showing no regard for the majesty and holiness of the Almighty, and brazenly desecrating and blaspheming everything traditionally sacred. He shall seek to "wear out the saints of the Most High," which means that terror and torture will be used to get them to deny their Lord. Modern brainwashing techniques in current godless countries are at least similar to this cruel attack upon God's people. And he will "think to change the times and the law." This means that the Antichrist will put his own stamp upon his era, and that he will set up moral and legal norms consistent with his own evil nature and in opposition to those of the Scriptures. He will not merely try to do this, but will actually succeed (v. 25b).

After a comparatively brief reign (vs. 25b–28) the regime of the Antichrist will come to an abrupt end. Daniel already knew of the throne of God and its supremacy (v. 9). He knew that God really directs all things, never losing his sovereign and just control over everything, including the great forces of unrighteousness. World events are not dependent upon the actions and decrees of beast-like men, no matter how monstrous their power, but upon the ultimate rule of God, the Almighty One. Before His throne the crowned and the uncrowned, great and small, must appear when the divine court opens sessions and the heavenly records are opened (vs. 9, 10). Let us fear God!

We might try to summarize the impressions created by Daniel's dream in chapter 7. The line runs from Nebuchadnezzar to Cyrus to Alexander to Rome. These are characterized by pride, the lust for power, world-wide rulership, and world oppression. Chapter 7 differs from chapter 2 in that chapter 2 gives us a pictorial description of the lust for imperial rule, chapter 7 gives us a characterization or interpretation of it. The message is plain: out of Babel comes Satan in all his anger, exercising his influence and effecting his terrible designs by way of expanding power unto world dominion and world oppression. This is the very structure of apostate life, especially in the area of the important political sphere. Throughout this dispensation we must expect to see awful things, and the end is not yet. Only after the Antichrist has come into power with all the terrible consequences that implies can we look for His appearing. Come, Lord Jesus!

## Questions for Discussion

1. The Belgic Confession (Art. V) says that, "the very blind are able to perceive that the things foretold in them are being fulfilled." Can you illustrate this in connection with Daniel 7?
2. Does this chapter take a dim view of the authority and validity of human government?
3. Can you see in the revelation of the ten horns an explanation of the fact that world-wide dominion has not yet been realized in this age?
4. Do you think that there is evident in the revolutionary student and other movements of today any kind of fulfillment of Daniel 7?
5. Do you believe that the Bible teaches that the anti-Christian movement in history will come to expression in the reign of a single world emperor, the Antichrist?
6. What does II Thessalonians 2:8 say about the Antichrist?
7. Does the inevitable appearance of Antichrist render impossible or undesirable the pursuit of a truly Christian political movement?
8. What does it mean that "the books were opened" in connection with the appearance of the Great Judge in verses 9 and 10? Should we fear that judgment?

# Daniel's Perspective with Respect to the End-Time of the Captivity

*Daniel 8*

**Daniel's Vision in Chapter 8:1–17**

From our lesson topic you can gather that we interpret this chapter to be a revelation from God to Daniel concerning the nature of the time at the close of the period in which Jerusalem is in captivity. Prophetically this end-time period corresponds to the time of the Antichrist at the end of our age. In other words, we see in chapter 8 something which ought to have great interest for us as we take note of the lateness of the hour on God's clock of prophecy.

We assume that Daniel was actually in Susa, perhaps on a political mission. There in a vision (distinguished from the dream by virtue of the fact that it took place while the prophet was awake), Daniel sees the awesome attack of the ram and the he-goat. The he-goat is totally victorious, but his reign lasts but a little while and he is replaced by four other "horns." Out of one of these comes a fastgrowing horn, who is a mortal enemy of the true worship of God. His reign, says "a holy one," will endure 2,300 evenings and mornings before the sanctuary is restored. When Daniel sees this he is given to hear the interpretation by the angel Gabriel, who assures him that "the vision is for the time of the end."

### The Heavenly Interpretation of the Vision; 8:18–27

The interpretation is not difficult, since we are told explicitly that the ram with the two horns is Medo-Persia, and the he-goat is Alexander the Great of Greece. Cyrus the Persian united the Medes and the Persians into a great empire which lasted for a couple of centuries. When Alexander (356–323 B.C.) died, four kingdoms came into existence: Macedonia, Thrace, Egypt, and Syria.

The "little horn" of verse 9 and the king of the "bold countenance" of verse 23 is the antichrist of the Old Testament, Antiochus Epiphanes. He is represented as very clever, powerful, terribly destructive, successful, hostile to all people of renown (he hates God-ordained distinctions!) and the saints of God, cunning and deceitful, obsessed with his own greatness, ruthless, and an enemy of God and His anointed. Thus his proud name which literally means, "the divine king of Syria." History tells us that he acted as these specifications indicate, and that his rule (175–163 B.C.) was marked by the unbelievable hypocrisy and deceit predicted of this hitherto unequaled enemy of God's cause and people.

The climax of the godless rule of this Old Testament antichrist is reached when he stops the daily sacrifice in Jerusalem and, out of unqualified hatred for God, offers a sacrifice of swine flesh to Zeus in the Lord's holy temple! In this and other ways, says Daniel, truth was cast down to the ground (v. 12). The ceremonies of Israel's religion had been given by God to demonstrate the need for atonement, that which could only come by the suffering and death of the Son of God, the promised Messiah.

All of this takes place in connection with a great apostasy among the people of God. Under the influence of Greek culture the Jewish people were secularized. To be *secular* simply means that one lives and works for the things that are worldly and temporal, rather than for the heavenly and the eternal. By experts (for example, Harvey Cox in

*The Secular City)* we, today, on this continent have been
labeled as uniquely *secular*! Antiochus Epiphanes furthered
the cause of this secularization by giving preferential
treatment to those Jews who were minded to adopt the
ideas and ways of the Greeks. Those who resisted this
abandonment of the true religion in favor of the Greeks
were persecuted. This was done by taking away from them
that which was most precious to them, the daily sacrifice.
Prophetically this points to the last days of our time when
the church will become worldly and persecution will be the
lot of the faithful.

This anti-Christian regime will last but a short time
(2,300 days). This is a symbolical figure, which means that
this kingdom will endure for a very specific time, but that it
will be cut off abruptly. The idea of a definite, completed
period is to be found in the number *thousand*, its specification
in the fact that it is *two thousand*, and the abruptness of its
end in the number, three hundred (less than one-third of a
thousand). God's people are always comforted to know that
the duration of the enemy's rule is fixed by God, and will be
terminated by him after but a little while.

Daniel is told that Antiochus Epiphanes would come to an
end which would be brought about by God Himself. "By no
human hand, he shall be broken" (v. 25). It is not known
just how he died. An ancient historian tells us that he
passed away after a 12-year reign as a completely demented
person. Another Jewish source says that he died in bed
while suffering from an unusually severe torture of
conscience. God Himself destroyed him, and plunged him
into hellish agonies without the aid of anyone. This is an
end similarly predicted for the last Antichrist.

It is noteworthy that the chapter twice mentions
Daniel's reaction to the things that are shown him. In the
first instance he is overwhelmed by the appearance of the
angel Gabriel. In fact, he cannot help falling into a deep

sleep (not out of boredom but out of inability to bear up under the burden of coming into contact with a heavenly emissary), and Gabriel must arouse him. We must not forget that man has fallen so deeply from his original state that his nerves cannot stand to communicate with angels.
The heavenly climate is so heavily laden with holiness that it is too much even for a man as saintly as Daniel to endure with comfort.

The second instance picturing Daniel's reaction is found in the last verse in which we read that he "was appalled by the vision and did not understand it." By this the prophet means to say that the things he has been given to know were enough to make one pale with fright, and that they were of such a nature that one could not reduce them to some simple logical pattern of explanation. This does not mean that they were incapable of being read, but that the things revealed were uniquely divine in character, and therefore altogether different than anything we might expect or devise. To illustrate: the end of the anti-Christian horror perpetrated by Antiochus Epiphanes is not the birth of Jesus Christ. Between this godless ruler and the Prince of Peace is more than 150 years. And during that time Israel is not removed from the storm and tumult of the world sea, but left right within it. When the Lord Jesus is born He finds His people in another, even more severe subjugation, this time under Rome, the fourth beast!

There are two thoughts with which we close this comment on Daniel 8:

> 1. The grace of God in Christ Jesus does not come up out of the history which is prophetically portrayed here. It comes in spite of it. It is pure grace, that is, the undeserved and not expected goodness of the God of all mercy.

2. In the history of the world God's people are often asked to wait out long periods of chaos and confusion in which things seem to be going very badly for the indestructible Kingdom of God. The one woe passes, and it is followed by another which is even worse. No wonder that we are called to be patient and believing! And, from this chapter we learn that the patience of the saints does end in triumph.

## Questions for Discussion

1. Why is Alexander the Great represented as a he-goat whose passage is so swift that it appears as if he is moving "without touching the ground?"

2. Why is it said that the "little horn" which waxes great cast down "some of the host of the stars"?

3. Why would Antiochus Epiphanes make such a great issue out of the destruction of the temple-worship? What is the relationship between the daily sacrifice ("the continual burnt offering") and the cross of Christ? and the means of grace (the preaching of the Word and administration of the sacraments)?

4. Who is the man who speaks to Gabriel in verse 16?

5. Why is Antiochus Epiphanes called "a man of bold countenance?"

6. Is there any relationship between the hatred of Antiochus Epiphanes for truth and his practice of dishonesty and the current indifference of many in the Church for instruction in sound doctrine?

7. Does the injunction "seal up the vision" (v. 26) mean that Daniel might not tell anyone of this vision? If not, why not?

# The Heavenly Perspective with Respect to the Coming of Christ

*Daniel 9*

### Daniel's Prayer; 9:1–21

Daniel's faithfulness in prayer is something we have noted before (ch. 6). This ninth chapter gives us a wonderful insight into the importance and nature of believing prayer, a lesson we can afford to learn and re-learn! Daniel's unusually great significance does not stem from his diplomatic wisdom so much as the fact that he is an intercessor for his people. It is to such intercessors (most prominently, Jesus Christ, *the* intercessor at God's right hand!) that the Church owes so much. We shall not experience the revival and reformation we so desperately need if such "prayer warriors" cannot be enlisted in this great service.

It is of key importance to our interpretation of this chapter to note that the angelic messenger is Gabriel, who also appears in a similar capacity in chapter 8, and who appears in Luke 1:26 as the herald of the birth of our Savior to the Virgin Mary. In this chapter Daniel's prayer is answered by God with a prophetic description of the time between Daniel and the coming of our Lord at Bethlehem, and the fall of Jerusalem (70 A.D.).

Chapters 8 and 9 are closely related, although their messages are quite opposite in character. Both deal with the post-exilic period, the time after the Captivity until the birth of Christ. In chapter 8 we see this as a time of wrath and judgment, a kind of end-time in which we see the filling up of the remains of Israel's sufferings as a type of Christ.

In chapter 9 we see the sunshine of God's redeeming love in Christ Jesus. These chapters complement each other, revealing to us that history moves between the poles of God's wrath and God's reconciliation, between divine rejection and acceptance.

The most prominent features of Daniel's prayer might be:

1. His identification of himself with God's cause. He is not primarily concerned with his own affairs, but with the fact that the name of God is being blasphemed because of the rejection and the captivity of Israel.

2. His deep humiliation in which he sees that the shameful situation of God's people is not to be sought in the cruelty of Babylon but in the sins of himself and his people and their leaders.

3. His appeal to God as the Covenant God who has identified Himself with His Church as it came to expression in His city, His holy hill, His sanctuary, His people called by His Name, all of which is a direct result of His sovereign mercy.

### Gabriel's Answer from God; 9:22–27

Daniel's prayer was prompted by something which he read in the Scriptures, more specifically in Jeremiah 25:11, 12 and 29:10, to this effect: "the number of years which... must pass before the end of the desolations of Jerusalem, namely, seventy years." Please remember that Jerusalem for Daniel never lost its importance or his deepest affection. Daniel understood that the way in which God dispenses His grace is the way of his tabernacle, the place where Immanuel ("God with us") dwells, where His atonement is recognized as the only basis for our redemption.

The destruction of Jerusalem and the interruption of its temple-service was of crucial significance for Daniel, therefore. The seventy years which Daniel found in Jeremiah's prophecy must be taken literally. From the Fall of Assyria (609 B.C.) to the Fall of Babylon (539 B.C.) is seventy years, very likely the period to which Jeremiah refers. Jeremiah does not say that Judah would be in captivity for seventy years, but rather that the nations would be in subjection to Babylon for that length of time, after which Israel would return. Israel's actual captivity was something like 58 years.

Although the historical reference here is to be taken literally, there is a symbolic significance in the use of the number *seventy*. Seventy is 10 times 7, and the number *seven* is the basic figure. It is the total of 3 plus 4, or, of God (the Triune God) and the world ("the four corners of the earth"). Seven has been called "the Immanuel number," the number which symbolically represents the presence of God with us. Multiplied by ten we see the fullness and the perfection of God's victorious grace in Jesus Christ. The number *seventy* was for Daniel a ray of sunshine in the darkness of the world's night, by which he could see that the joyful sound of the Gospel did penetrate through all the noise of a wicked, imperial dictatorship.

Gabriel gives a direct response from God to Daniel's prayer. In fact, Daniel stresses that the answer came even while he was praying, from God's messenger who came to him "in swift flight at the time of the evening sacrifice." Verse 24 tells us that Daniel must know that a period of "seventy weeks of years" will take place after which the Messianic, official service will be accomplished. We understand this verse to mean that after a time whose length and whose purpose is governed by God's decree the Lord Jesus will appear, in and through whom the Church and Kingdom will be established in the way of atonement for sin.

Verse 25 serves to tell Daniel that Jerusalem shall be restored. From the time that God gave the word to restore and build Jerusalem (the word in Jer. 25:11, 12) until the edict of Cyrus giving the Jews the liberty to restore the Temple is "seven weeks." This is a rounded off, God-decreed period which will end in that edict. After that there will be 62 weeks during which the reconstruction will be accomplished, but it will be a "troubled time." This was literally fulfilled in Israel's history: the difficulties and dangers in the time of rebuilding, in the time of Ahasuerus, from the side of the very worldly Greek culture, in the time of Antiochus Epiphanes and the Roman domination — all of this indicates that Israel was continuously threatened by the power and influence of world rulers and heathen culture.

Verse 26 refers to the Lord Jesus Christ ("an anointed one"), who is represented in terms of His suffering. This suffering is undeserved, for there is nothing against Him. The city whose destruction is predicted is Jerusalem (70 A.D.), which will be overcome by the flood of God's wrath (cf. Nah. 1:8).

Verse 27 is best interpreted, we feel, if it is seen to refer to the Coming of Christ, the Head of the Covenant of Grace. In the week of His coming He will by His ministry and sacrifice confirm the covenant for many. In the middle of a week, that is, abruptly, will the Old Testament sacrifice and offerings be brought to a finish. The last half of the verse refers again to the destruction of Jerusalem. That which God has decreed shall take place, so that the predicted desolation is realized in the way of His judgment.

Reviewing the whole of this chapter, we see that it is God's answer to Daniel's prayer concerning the restoration of Israel and its temple-service. The answer goes far beyond the prayer. God's thoughts are higher than our thoughts!

So in the New Testament, thanks to the Spirit of Romans 8:26ff., the prayers of the Church have a scope far beyond the knowledge of the believers. This does not make their prayers less urgent, but rather intensifies the need for prayer. The essence of this chapter is not exhausted in the prophecy of Jerusalem's fall, but in the coming of the promised Savior. In and through the channel of Israel's history flows God's great salvation, and this river reaches to all the nations.

### Questions for Discussion

1. How does the Heidelberg Catechism (Lord's Day 45) describe the need for prayer?
2. How does Bible-reading and prayer relate in Daniel 9?
3. Is it at all necessary to demonstrate our sorrow for sin in such an extreme manner as is done by Daniel in chapter 9?
4. Daniel appeals to God's mercy and to God's self-interest ("thy city and thy people are called by thy name," v. 19); is this the right thing to do in prayer?
5. What is the significance of the Covenant for prayer?
6. Is it always true that God is so eager to answer prayer as Gabriel's swift coming to Daniel indicates?
7. Why does Scripture refer so often to the destruction of Jerusalem? Is the present rise and development of Israel something to be viewed with special interest and appreciation by Christians?
8. Should Christians feel that Israel's role in history is finished, or that it must still factor in some special way before the return of the Savior?

*Lesson 10*

# The Struggle for Judah in the Heavenlies

*Daniel 10*

**Introductory Remarks**

Chapters 10, 11, and 12 of Daniel comprise a single prophetic experience. They reveal to Daniel that a mighty warfare goes on in heaven, and that the struggle between the Kingdom of God and the kingdoms of this world is not isolated from that conflict. Especially in chapter 10 do we see something of that which is going on in the (for us) invisible world of the spirits. Chapter 10 begins by referring to "the third year of Cyrus, king of Persia." Cyrus is the king who gave permission for the Jews to return to Palestine. Chapter 10 takes place a few years after this return, and is concerned with the welfare of Jerusalem and of them who are there to restore the holy city. Daniel was left behind, not because he preferred it that way, but because God had a task for him to perform.

**Daniel Sees A Visitor; 10:2–9**

Chapter 10 takes place in the first month of the year (corresponding to our March), a time of festivity in honor of the god of gods, Marduk. The prophet is "on vacation" during that time, abstains from the worship of the false god, and, while everyone else is giving expression to play and merriment, retires to fast and pray, not merely for devotional reasons, but because of his concern for Judah.

The occasion for his mourning is the state of affairs among them who have returned to Judah. It is estimated that about 200,000 returned (men, women, and children). This was but a remnant of the number that had been taken into captivity, and was not the more successful or prominent of the Jews living away from Jerusalem. These were the spiritually-minded nucleus, for whom return was very desirable. However, the group was not strong, and the earlier experiences in Palestine were very discouraging. There was spiritual weakness within the group, due to the influence of decades of residence in a heathen land (many of the wives were of heathen origin), and there was resistance from without (cf. Ezra 3, 4). All of this hampered the reformation in Jerusalem, and this really troubled Daniel.

There were other avenues of influence open to Daniel, for he was a great man in one of the greatest empires of the world, but he turns to the one which is open to every believer, no matter how small he might be in the kingdom of heaven. That is the avenue of *prayer*. His prayer is not routine, formal, or perfunctory; it is fervent, James 5:16. Daniel fasts in order that he might concentrate upon that task which is prayer, and in order that he might plead the cause of his people with the God of heaven.

We visualize the course of events this way: Daniel has finished his vacation and is on his way back to the capital city, accompanied by a caravan of assistants, soldiers, etc. Suddenly an angel appears in dazzling, radiant appearance. Those with Daniel see nothing, but sense the awesomeness of the event and flee. He is a mighty messenger, equipped for battle, holy, and fearful to behold. Daniel's strength ebbs away, and he sinks into a deep coma. By his prayers Daniel has moved heaven itself to action, but contact with the heavenly messenger is a terribly disconcerting experience.

### The Heavenly Messenger's Message; 10:10–11:1

The outstanding fact in the angel's message is that he had left the presence of God some three weeks earlier, but arrived only then. During the intervening period it must have seemed to Daniel that God was no longer minded to hear his prayers. The agony of this experience for Daniel may be compared to that which our Lord experienced on the cross when He suffered the abandonment of the Father (the comparison must be limited to the type-antitype relationship). But now Daniel learns something which every praying Christian must realize, namely, that God had heard, had dispatched help, but that there were other things that had to take place before this might be seen. It is a biblically established fact that God is a hearer of prayers, and we must resolutely believe this — even if we do not see the evidence in our time.

But why did it take the angel twenty-one days to reach Daniel? The angel explains that "the prince of the king-dom of Persia" resisted him for that length of time. This is not the king of Persia, but an evil angel, a mighty spirit out of hell. He intercepted the good angel, possible because angels also are subject to time and space. The battle was spiritual in character, a word-battle, in which the anti-Christian genius which infected and motivated the Persian empire was defended over against Daniel's right to be heard by God as His "beloved." The issue was the righteousness of God as He seeks to bless His elect, lead them to glory, and render them acceptable in his sight upon the basis of the promised atonement.

It is the time *before* the birth and sacrifice of the Christ, and so the battle could not be brought to easy victory by God's angel. He needed help, and so the faithful and powerful Michael comes to his aid. Michael stays on in the arena of the spiritual warfare, and his colleague goes to find Daniel. This cooperation indicates the oft-repeated biblical description of the angelic world, both good and evil, as well-organized. Apparently some among the demons are assigned certain specific areas of concern, in this instance the political empire of Persia.

Daniel is told that this struggle continues unabated throughout history. After Persia's downfall another anti-Christian world-power will arise in Greece. Fact is, Daniel is told that things will get worse. The influence of Greece was most dangerous for the Church since it represented a more cultural and philosophical opposition. Persia was rather limited, being another heathen, brutal power. Greece was more subtle, offering attractive ideas which did not seem to be so seriously incompatible with God's Word, but which were actually most devastating for God's people.

Please note that when the angel speaks to Daniel he recovers his strength and his courage. This effect is characteristic of God's Word, and is an indication of the fact that the Christian must not try to live apart from the ministry of the Word. The Word is a power, indeed, and it gives strength to those who hear it in faith.

The angel says that he is telling Daniel things out of "the book of truth" (v. 21). This is not the Bible insofar as it was then available, but rather the book of God's counsel or sovereign decree, God's counsel is His plan, the eternally established and existing plan of salvation and history. Please note that although the angel knows of this predestinating plan of God he is not fatalistic or passive. This is because the zeal of the faithful is not geared to the possibility of triumph or defeat, but to the actuality of God's will and the deep desire to serve its grand purpose, namely, God's glory.

Why does the angel say that only Michael helps him in this struggle? Does not Jesus say "that the Father has legions of angels?" The answer is that their service has very definite limits. Its limit is to prevent the demonic frustration of God's redemptive plan, which is to save His people *in the way of suffering*. They are to keep the measure of that suffering within proper bounds, to render the opposition helpless beyond a certain point, and to serve God's counsel so that the salvation through the cross of Christ may surely take place.

We ought again to note that Satan has a peculiar interest in the Church, and in the politics of the world. These seem to us to be quite separate from each other, although the modern church shows great interest in current matters of international diplomacy and in all problems of social inequity. There is in our time a great revival of "the social gospel"! The truth is, of course, that Persia and Greece are inspired of the Evil One in order to destroy the people of God. That is their "real meaning" in Daniel's prophecy. It is true that Satan's first concern is always the downfall of the godly. And it is likewise true that Satan knows that the great political movements are very effective as instrumentalities to embarrass and harass God's children.

The comforting message of the chapter is that the good angels will care for us, and that the victory of Christ over anti-Christian powers is assured. This was the answer to Daniel's prayer, and this was the answer to ours as well. Our posture before God must be the same as Daniel's, however. Of us, too, the angels must be able to say, "you set your mind to understand and humbled yourself before your God" (v. 12, RSV).

### Questions for Discussion

1. Why is the angel dressed so luxuriously if they are humble servants of God?
2. Can you find comparisons between Daniel 10 and its description of the angel with the description of Jesus Christ in Revelation 1:12–16? Is it possible that the angel of Daniel 10 is the Angel of the LORD (the Christ of the Old Testament)?

3. Was it sin for so many of the Jews to stay back in the heathen world rather than to return to Palestine?

4. Why did the people of the area wish recognition and participation in the work of the temple- and city-restoration in Jerusalem?

5. How must we conceive of the relationship of the angelic world to ours, and what is the influence of that world upon ours?

6. Is there a special demon in charge of Washington? Moscow? Chicago? Grand Rapids?

7. If there was a demonic influence at work with respect to Greece, why do so many prize and praise the culture which developed there?

8. How could it be possible for Daniel to serve the LORD better in Persia than in Jerusalem?

9. What comfort did Daniel derive from the angel's revelation?

# The Struggle for Judah on Earth

*Daniel 11*

### The History Prior to the Antichrist; 11:2–20

The last two chapters of Daniel are two of the most difficult in the Book, and perhaps in all the Bible. Reading these chapters we often run stuck as we try to interpret. It is not possible to do more than to indicate the main lines and principal features of that which is here revealed.

In his second letter to the Thessalonians Paul reminds us that the return of Christ in glory shall not take place until the "man of sin" appears. This "man of sin" is the Antichrist. It might be helpful if we summarize the biblical characteristics of the Antichrist as follows:

1. The Antichrist is not Satan himself, but an embodiment and instrument of Satan.

2. The Antichrist is a human being in whom a satanic spiritual movement hostile to Jesus Christ finds its consummation.

3. The antichrist movement is not limited to a single appearance, but is evident in a series of appearances throughout history. These appearances serve as forerunners of the final, great manifestation of the Antichrist, "the Beast," just prior to Christ's second coming.

4. The Antichrist is head of a kingdom, a realm which is in part spiritual (the false church) and in part imperial (the false kingdom).

5. In an effort to mislead men the Antichrist deliberately shows a resemblance to Christ.

6. The Antichrist does signs and wonders, by which he makes propaganda for himself, II Thessalonians 2:9.

Just as Christ has His types in history (Melchizedek, Joseph, David, etc.) in whom His coming and character are revealed, so also the Antichrist has his forerunners. In the perspective of Daniel's prophecy this is especially the awful Antiochus Epiphanes, about whom we have spoken earlier. In Daniel 11 the portrait of this fierce opponent of God's people is drawn in order that we might easier recognize the Antichrist whenever and wherever we see him.

The first twenty verses of Daniel 11 give us a representation of the time before the appearance of the Antichrist, or, in this instance, of the coming of Antiochus Epiphanes, the antichrist of the Old Testament. The main emphasis of this section is that the time prior to the final appearance of the Antichrist will be one of great confusion, of blood and tears. It is perhaps impossible to apply with complete certainty the details of these verses in terms of actual history, although certain indications and identifications have been made with... some plausibility. For our purpose it is enough to see just the main emphases.

There are a few important ideas that we should note before passing on to the last part of the chapter. We might summarize these as follows:

1. The Bible does not furnish its readers with detailed history in advance, and therefore it does not identify the persons, peoples, cities, and nations of which it speaks.

Believers must "live by faith," even though they do know with absolute certainty such facts as:

(a) God is the LORD of history.

(b) He directs all things to serve His purposes.

(c) His people may believe that the Kingdom of God will triumph.

2. The coming of the Antichrist is not traceable to the character of the world empires, but is explainable only in terms of the existence of, him who is the Savior and Lord, King Jesus. In Daniel 11 we read of two kinds of kingdoms, one which may be called a "welfare state," and the other a "reign of brute strength." Neither of these *produces* the Antichrist. Daniel is given to see that basic to and behind all else is the struggle of Genesis 3:15, out of which will arise the indestructible Kingdom of God.

## The Appearance of the Antichrist; 11:21–45

In the second part of Daniel 11 we read of the appearance of Antiochus Epiphanes, the antichrist of the Old Testament. Every detail of this section is not applicable to the Antichrist. Daniel's prophecy is rather one of broad strokes on a large canvas, by which we are given to see that although the Antichrist will rule successfully, his reign will be characterized by the same features as those found in history generally.

The motif of his reign will be "security," verses 21, 24, and "prosperity," verse 36. In the interest of a happy, prosperous, safe life *in this world outside of Jesus Christ* men will follow his direction and serve him. Security and prosperity are not really material or political matters, but spiritual, and so the godless world will seek solution to its gnawing problems by appeal to the Antichrist.

The character of the Antichrist will be one of general contemptibility (from the viewpoint of faith, of course). He will be a deceiver, a "flatterer" a clever manipulator. To get along in his world requires loyalty and allegiance to him, which means great hardship for the faithful people of God.

The outstanding characteristic of the Antichrist will be his ungodliness. He will bring all his wrath to bear on the sanctuary and the holy covenant. In the place of the true religion he puts the adoration and worship of himself as the great world-ruler. By this description (cf. vs. 32–36) Daniel means to emphasize that the real issue in all of this is the love and service of Jesus Christ, intolerable to Satan and the world under his dominion.

The expression in verse 37, "nor the desire of women," is of special significance. This is one of the things which the Antichrist shall not "regard," that is, hold in high and holy esteem. I understand this to be a reference to the fact that he is the lawless one who tramples upon every ordinance of God, even the creational ordinance of marriage. The biblical pronouncement of Genesis 3:16 with respect to the woman ("and thy desire shall be to thy husband, and he shall rule over thee,") will be resisted and rejected by the Antichrist. This is a sample of the total apostasy and degeneration of his rule.

From the conclusion of the chapter (vs. 40–45) two things may be seen:

> 1. The Antichrist will conquer the world in such a manner that the words of John will be fulfilled ("and the whole world wondered after the beast." Rev. 13:3). The Antichrist will give the impression of great glory and unlimited power, causing all men to stand amazed!

> 2. At the very peak of his power the Antichrist will come to an abrupt end. by the intervention of Jesus

Christ, who will come upon the clouds of heaven. The appearance of the Antichrist is not due to developments within the world, for he appears suddenly and unexpectedly. He relates to the Evil One and hell and to the demonic forces rather than to men as such. And his defeat is likewise sudden and catastrophic, the result of the work of the Lord Jesus Christ, whose grace is similarly unexpected and unlikely except for the sovereign goodness of God.

The great comfort for us is that Jesus Christ and His birth in Bethlehem was not prevented by the Antichrist of the Old Testament, Antiochus Epiphanes. So the return of our Lord will not be frustrated by the appearance of the great man of sin, the great Antichrist.

**Questions for Discussion**
1. How large a place in our thinking as New Testament Christians should the Antichrist occupy? Is this not a morbid, sickly idea?
2. How do you evaluate the fact that there is a parallelism between the pattern of Old Testament and New Testament events?
3. Do you see any relationship between the modern immorality and the things said of Antichrist in Daniel 11:37? What about "situational ethics" and this prophecy?
4. There are dire predictions abroad today with respect to the future of the established church; do these predictions relate in any way to the anti-Christian movement?
5. Does Daniel rule out the possibility of a genuine world peace? Can a Christian be a pacifist?

# The Struggle for Judah Governed by God's Decree

*Daniel 12*

## Introduction

Daniel 12 closes the Book of Daniel. It is of the nature of an epilogue, that is, a word of explanation after the play or drama is over. We must remember that throughout the Book the point at issue is the conflict between Jerusalem and the world, the God-ordained struggle of Genesis 3:15. This is especially true in chapters 10–12. God preaches His Gospel of salvation and victory for His people through His servant Daniel. He does this in such a way as to instruct and comfort the faithful. There is no consolation for the ungodly or satisfaction for the merely curious in Daniel's revelations. Daniel and his believing brothers and sisters in this time must continue to live by faith in the God whose Kingdom is indestructible.

## Protection and Glory; vs. 1–4

The announcement that Michael, the great angelic prince, will defend the people of God in the great crises of history means that the Christian has heavenly resources upon which he may draw as he seeks to stand in the day of battle. The real Protector of God's people is Jesus Christ, but He uses the angels in this service. For this the believer prays, if his prayer is scriptural.

The description of the resurrection does not apply to the time of Antiochus Epiphanes, of course, but to the end of the New Testament age. This is typical of Old Testament prophecy, namely, that it draws lines directly from any part of history to the end. Bible prophecy sees the end from the beginning, and all things in the light of that hoped for, glorious consummation.

In the last judgment some go to glory, others to perdition. All are in the resurrection. Those who are lost bear the impress of the Antichrist, that is, shame and contempt. The saved are represented as wise soul-winners. They "turn many to righteousness," which means that their influence is toward obedience and godliness. Their glory is spectacular, for they will shine as the stars in the sky.

The command that Daniel "shut up the words and seal the book" does not mean that he must keep it secret, but that it must be valued and preserved as a precious gem so that God's people may draw comfort and instruction therefrom in the day of need. The obligation of the believer to search and study the Scriptures is expressly stated (v. 4). This is a very serious and urgent Christian calling which we tend to forget. It seems as if many wish to own an easy-to-understand religion nowadays, and they do not care for sermons which demand close attention or for a church membership which places any difficult burdens of responsibility upon them. Those who will not heed this call to Bible study will easily fall prey to the Antichrist, the false prophet!

### The Fulfillment of God's Counsel; vs. 5–13

Daniel sees one more revelation from God, this time in the form of three angels, one on each side of the river, and one in between, standing "above the waters." The question that is raised is as to the time when the terrible things Daniel has been given to see prophetically will end. This vision is intended to be of comfort for the people of God in his and subsequent times.

The general features of the revelation furnished are:

1. With great solemnity the messenger speaks in terms of an oath, indicating that his message is one which comes from the God of truth, whose Word is to be trusted (v. 7).

2. The expression, "a time, and times, and a half," occurs more often in prophetic parts of Scripture. It means to indicate that the period to which reference is made is complete (therefore it may seem to be very long from our point of view), and yet that it comes to an abrupt end when it pleases God to bring things to conclusion. God will fulfill His counsel, His decree, and will yet guard the welfare of His chosen ones.

3. Daniel is told that throughout this period the elect will be saved, the unbelieving will continue in their foolishness (v. 10). The gathering of the Church by our Lord Jesus Christ cannot be frustrated by the most violent efforts of Satan and the Antichrist.

4. The number, "a thousand two hundred and ninety days," is a symbolical number. Please note that it is days, not years or even months, meaning that the time is actually short. Also: although the period is complete (so that God's counsel is fully realized therein), it is cut off before it reaches the round number of 1,300. God will interrupt in the interest of His own.

5. Thus, the number, "thousand three hundred and five and thirty days," is the one to which the believer by faith attaches himself. This is not only a kind of complete number, but one which ends by marking success toward the realization of the perfect rest. This is to be seen in the fact that 1,300 is reached plus 35, which is one half of 70, a number partaking of the full

Sabbath rest, but not yet fully reaching that level. The number 70 will not be reached until the end when the Lord brings about the resurrection of vs. 1–4.

6. Believers are to be characterized by two things: faithful ongoing in duty and perfect confidence in the Lord's promised mercy. Daniel is told to go his way (vs. 9, 13), which means that he should continue to walk in the ways which he has been going. One can easily understand that Daniel must often have wondered if his policies and principles were really worthwhile. He had turned his back upon the world's pleasures (readily available to him in their every form as a great world ruler), and he had sought the realities of the Kingdom of God. These words of assurance must have been very precious to him! He is told that he will reach his reward, and in it he will stand at the end of the days.

## Questions for Discussion

1. Do you think that Daniel knew anything of what we know as the doctrine of the resurrection from the dead?
2. Why are believers called "the wise" in this chapter?
3. How do you understand verse 11 of Daniel 12?
4. What is the concrete significance of a Christian's "waiting" in verse 12?
5. How do you relate the Book of Daniel and the Book of Revelation?
6. Do you think that we pay enough attention to the more prophetic books of the Bible in our time?
7. How would you summarize the message of the Book of Daniel?

# Notes